Building Powerful
Learning Environments

Building Powerful Learning Environments

From Schools to Communities

Arina Bokas

ROWMAN & LITTLEFIELD
Lanham • Boulder • New York • London

Published by Rowman & Littlefield
A wholly owned subsidiary of The Rowman & Littlefield Publishing Group, Inc.
4501 Forbes Boulevard, Suite 200, Lanham, Maryland 20706
www.rowman.com

Unit A, Whitacre Mews, 26-34 Stannary Street, London SE11 4AB

British Library Cataloguing in Publication Information Available

Library of Congress Cataloging-in-Publication Data

Names: Bokas, Arina, 1972–
Title: Building powerful learning environments : from schools to communities /
    Arina Bokas.
Description: Lanham, Maryland : Rowman & Littlefield, 2017. | Includes
    bibliographical references and index.
Identifiers: LCCN 2016037776 (print) | LCCN 2016037837 (ebook) |
    ISBN 9781475830927 (cloth : alk. paper) | ISBN 9781475830934 (pbk. : alk. paper) |
    ISBN 9781475830941 (Electronic)
Subjects: LCSH: Home and school. | Classroom environment.
Classification: LCC LC225 .B595 2017 (print) | LCC LC225 (ebook) | DDC
    371.19—dc23
LC record available at https://lccn.loc.gov/2016037776

♾™ The paper used in this publication meets the minimum requirements of American
National Standard for Information Sciences—Permanence of Paper for Printed Library
Materials, ANSI/NISO Z39.48-1992.

Printed in the United States of America

To my children, Sasha and Mark:
May your learning journeys never end.

Contents

List of Contributors

Acknowledgments

Every book has a story. Seemingly unconnected events, unrelated encounters, and everyday work come together one day to form the foundation for an idea—an idea that persists, grows, tests and refines itself, and then evolves into a flow of pages.

This book's story began five years ago at Bailey Lake Elementary in Clarkston, Michigan, with my casual decision to help a friend, Nina Brown, who was chairing a program at our children's school. My daughter had just started her second grade, and my son had begun his kindergarten year; thus, it was time to get involved.

As those who have volunteered at their children's schools might know, once you "get involved," you get involved. In a year, I became the school's parent–teacher association (PTA) president, then the president of our district's PTA Council two years later, followed by election to the Michigan PTA Nominating and Leadership Development Committee.

Over these years of service, I have had many opportunities to work at various levels of leadership. I produced my own television series, *The Future of Learning*, presented at conferences both nationally and internationally, and collaborated with parents and educators. I have come into contact with many remarkable individuals whose dedication to children and public education is worth nothing less than high admiration. These people are teachers, parents, school administrators, members of the community, and educational leaders.

It was because of the diversity of perspectives and influences that I was fortunate to experience firsthand that the idea of how we, as educators, parents, and community members, could function as "us" instead of "us and them" entered my mind. This idea persisted, grew, tested and refined itself, and filled the pages of this book.

First and foremost, I would like to acknowledge the very special role that Bailey Lake Elementary families, teachers, and staff have played in creating the nurturing soil and solid foundation for this book. Many ideas and practices reflected here stem from the collaborative work that took place at Bailey Lake Elementary.

Among many talented educators at Bailey Lake and Clarkston Schools in general, there are two people who have been instrumental in developing the concept of a culture of partnerships. Meredith Copland, my son's second-grade teacher and now also a friend, colleague, and contributor to this book, was the first person with whom I shared my then far-fetched ideas for partnering with parents. In itself, her willingness to listen to a parent and try out these ideas in her classroom was a testament to a learning-oriented partnership that could exist between parents and teachers.

This could not have been possible, however, without principal Glenn Gualtieri, his servant leadership, and openness to give a go to something new. Not only did his continuous support enable me to develop my ideas further but it also created collaboration in building family–school partnerships in our school.

I am also indebted to Glenn as well as to my friend and PTA colleague Cheryl McNeil for reading the earlier version of my book and offering suggestions and comments. Cheryl's insights and probing questions were instrumental in shaping the content of this book.

My appreciation goes to Rod Rock, superintendent of Clarkston Schools, for opening the door to various opportunities and collaborations. In addition, over the past five years, the ideas presented here were influenced by many individuals with whom I had conversations about learning and continuity of a learning environment between schools and home. Among them are Sophie Sanders, Lisa Damone, Kara Cach, Mary Herzensteil, Kelly Teague, Sara Hoyle, Dena Pflieger, Dakotah Cooper, Michael Medvinsky, Julie Rains, Jennifer Johnson, Jessica Cleland, Robert Brazier, Blagica Taseski, Bethany Rocho, Renee Avery, Kathy Noble, and Megan Patnaude. Without them, this book would have substantially less to offer.

I am particularly grateful to my Rowman & Littlefield Education editor, Sarah Jubar, and her colleagues, as well as to the following educators who extended their help and advice leading to or during the project: Caryn Wells, Oakland University, MI; Jim Reese, Washington International School, Washington, DC; David Perkins, Harvard Graduate School of Education, MA; Odette Diaz Schuler, Center for the Advancement and Study of International Education, GA; and Laura Varlas, ASCD, VA.

In the actual writing of the book, I would like to acknowledge all of the contributors who took the time to share impressive examples of their work: Bonnie Lathram, Seattle, WA; Erika Lusky, Rochester, MI; Jennifer

Rossi and Adam Scher, Bloomfield Hills, MI; Georgina Ardalan and Terry Thomas, Washington, DC; Glenn Gualtieri, Meredith Copland, Michelle Simecek, and Howard Andress, Clarkston, MI; Jennifer Miller, Columbus, OH; and Marina Garcia, Macomb, MI.

Finally, there are my family and friends who have been supporting this book by affording me the time and space to write and by providing ongoing encouragement. Of special note are my husband, Gerald; close friends Kenneth Leavitt and Maggie Razdar; and children, Sasha and Mark—my continuous inspiration.

Preface

Learning environments . . . There is likely no educator who doesn't realize the importance of a learning environment and its impact on learning. As familiar as we might be with this concept, do we truly know who and what control it? Do learning environments change with time or do they conceptually stay the same? Do we just create them differently or understand them differently at different times?

For a long time, the thought has been that a learning environment is something that educators create and control within their schools and classrooms. However, many educators have come to understand that they cannot shoulder the entire burden of responsibility for student learning outcomes on their own; rather, it is necessary to expand a learning environment well beyond school walls and to embrace families, communities, other learning institutions, and businesses as vital stakeholders and co-builders of a learning environment.

School district leaders are trying various initiatives to re-imagine school–parent–community relationships, ranging from daily interactions to how district officials incorporate parents into decision-making processes. Educators are willing to share a responsibility for children's education with those whose actions they cannot always influence. What pushes them to embrace uncertainty and take a leap of faith by opening their classrooms and schools, while accepting that they can no longer educate alone? Perhaps the answer to it is in how the post-digital era shapes education and learning.

According to the president of *Getting Smart*, Tom Vander Ark's (2016, February 17) projection, based on research, emerging trends, and developments in technology and education, in twenty to thirty years, parents will be managers of their learners' profiles to ensure privacy and personalization. These profiles will be shared either partially or entirely with numerous learning providers of which schools will be one of many.

Most secondary learners will simultaneously engage with multiple providers, whereas advisors or learning coaches will serve individual families to
help with all of the learning options and postsecondary plans. Technology—
learner relationship management systems—will connect learners, advisors,
teachers, and parents through smart assistants. Businesses and organizations
will offer "short term project-based work experiences to youth while demonstrated knowledge and skills will contribute to competency-based progress as
well as portfolios and references" (para. 9).

This brings to our attention one rather obvious, but often overlooked, fact:
Learning is not limited to a classroom. It takes place anywhere any time. No
exceptions. Building on Vygotsky's (1978) idea that children grow into the
intellectual life that surrounds them (p. 88), we need to realize that this means
the intellectual life in its entirety. It is not enough for educators to think of a
child holistically at school; it is necessary to think of how to nurture holistic
learning environments anywhere a child spends his or her time, especially
at home. The extent to which twenty-first-century skills can be fostered in
students largely depends on a mindset of a community, and schools have to
lead the way by becoming the center of a new educational culture—a culture
of partnerships.

This book examines a need to shift our traditional paradigm of a learning
environment and to re-assign responsibilities. There is the two-fold message
here. First, there is no such thing as one isolated learning environment: Our
interconnected, complex world is a learning environment. Second, there is no
one person who can be responsible for the outcome of student learning in its
entirety, except for the learner himself or herself, when supported by all of
the learning environments he or she enters.

Along the way, it is necessary to realize that schools are responsible for
taking the first step in this direction. It cannot come from families or the community. It has to come from the entity that for the previous century and a half
has had the ultimate control over the education of U.S. youth. Educators and
school leaders have to share this control to impact a shift from the mindset of
"family engagement" to the mindset of "school–family–community partnerships," from seeing parents as schools' assistants at home to interacting with
them as colleagues and partners in their children's educational journey.

Released in October of 2015, an influential international reflection on
innovative learning environments by the Centre for Educational Research and
Innovation (Organization for Economic Co-Operation Development [OECD],
2015) brings to our attention the concept of learning ecosystems—interdependent combinations of species of various providers and organizations that
interact with learners over time and play various roles in their learning. The
report distinguishes three levels of learning environments: the micro level,
the meta level, and the mega level (p. 11). Using this as a foundation for

reframing the concept of a learning environment, I look into various levels of creating a new educational culture—a culture of partnerships—at district, school, and classroom levels.

The book provides practical guidance, strategies, and suggestions as well as conceptual understandings of why a change is necessary and what can be done to support it at various levels of educational leadership at each step of a culture of partnership formation. It offers examples and stories that capture the experiences of school leaders and teachers who took these ideas to heart and used them in their own schools to affect real change.

Introduction

How This Book Is Organized

The main body of this book consists of eight chapters and follows stages of a culture of partnerships formation, wherein strategies applicable to various levels of educational leadership (classrooms, schools, or districts) are discussed. Chapter 1 and chapter 2 create a foundation for understanding the rationale behind the necessity to re-envision and re-design a learning environment by taking stock of where we, as humankind, are at this time and place and how the dynamics of our times impact education.

Chapter 1 offers a brief look at the current state of education through the prism of how educational systems presently respond to the emerging twenty-first-century needs in the areas of job market and employment, global issues, and formation of individual self, agency, and purpose.

Chapter 2 poses a new set of questions that are defined by learning as opposed to the formal institutional system of schooling. It looks into the essence of individual learning and how it sketches the concept of a learning environment. It delineates two tiers of a learning environment—a micro level and a macro level—and examines the need to re-think responsibilities and controls in education. It invites educators to assess their own locus of control in their classrooms and schools.

Chapter 3 transitions to the concept of a culture of partnerships that is necessary to nurture a powerful learning environment. It explains an important shift that must occur in the mindsets of educators: from seeing parents as school helpers to interacting with them as colleagues in education of their children. It addresses such elements of this new educational culture as a shared vision, decision making, trust, and cultural forces (Ritchhart, 2015) as applied to a culture of partnerships. A number of key ideas and terminology are introduced in this chapter, including the three stages of a

1

culture of partnerships formation continuum: Creating Awareness, Seeking Engagement, and Supporting Collaboration.

Chapters 4 through 6 explore these three stages of a culture of partnerships formation. Chapter 4 is focused on how schools can create awareness—the first stage. It underscores the importance of intentionally designed systems for sharing education and learning-related information within a community. It addresses the questions of what content should be emphasized at this stage to promote learning awareness and what tools can be used by teachers and school leaders to this end. It also points out the most common obstacles to "getting through" to parents and community members and offers practical ways to overcome them. It provides educators with some resources and tools that they can try in their practices.

Chapter 5 brings to readers' attention the second—action based—stage of a culture of partnerships formation. The chapter addresses important shifts in thinking about how families and communities should be "engaged," insisting on moving away from simply using parental help in classroom assistance to providing families with learning opportunities and "letting them in." It provides concrete strategies and examples of effective practices for this type of parental engagement. It also brings attention to changes in schools' infrastructure that will allow them to expand their capacity for meaningful engagement of family and community members.

Chapter 6 explores the final stage where partnerships are being formed. It looks at various changes in the operating procedures and policies of schools and districts to allow partnerships to take root. It examines such important factors as training of staff and parent leaders, shared decision making and resources, as well as collaboration with school-affiliated organizations (e.g., parent–teacher associations), community organizations and businesses, and other learning organizations and environments outside of the local community.

Chapter 7 uncovers challenges of disadvantaged communities and families as well as of families with special needs learners, including special education and gifted children. It examines the three stages of a culture of partnerships formation, which are applied specifically to these groups.

Finally, chapter 8 features stories from various educators who share their examples of successful practices in moving toward partnerships with families and communities.

Of course, no book can completely answer all questions; nor can it outline one correct way to improve all learning environments and build family–school partnerships in all communities. Hopefully, this book can provide some guidance on how to approach these tasks. It offers strategies that worked for people in a variety of educational settings and can become a good resource for developing strategies that fit the needs of individual schools and districts.

Chapter One

The Fourth Industrial Revolution and Its Impact on Education

> All who have meditated on the art of governing mankind have been convinced that the fate of empires depends on the education of youth.
>
> —Aristotle

In the second decade of the twenty-first century, families, parent–teacher associations and organizations, homeschooling, and charter, private, and public schools are continuing a century-and-a-half-long competition for influence in the educational arena. For at least this long, families and schools have been co-existing in a strange and frustrating dichotomy. On the one hand, parents are decision makers in all of the affairs concerning their children; on the other hand, they are expected to forfeit this decision-making authority in matters related to one of the most vital areas of their children's growth and development: education.

Most schools realize that how a child learns in the classroom is largely determined by his or her family life and circumstances, but they often refuse to share their decision-making power with families, claiming the ultimate expertise in this field. Who should have the ultimate say over what and how a child learns—schools or families?

We, as humankind, are on the edge of a technological revolution that drastically changes the fundamentals of our lives, work, and personal and professional relationships. In its entirety and complexity, the change is unparalleled to any other transformation that humanity has undergone earlier. The Fourth Industrial Revolution, as Klaus Shwab (2016, January 14), founder and executive chairman of the World Economic Forum, defines our era, is continuing the trend of the digital revolution that has been occurring since the middle of the twentieth century and is "characterized by a fusion of technologies that is blurring the lines between the physical, digital, and biological spheres. [And

3

the response to it] must be integrated and comprehensive, involving all stake-holders of the global polity, from the public and private sectors to academia and civil society" (para. 1).

It is difficult to foresee all of the changes that need to occur in the field of education to meet the opportunities and challenges that the Fourth Industrial Revolution brings about, but something is already clear: Segregation, bound-aries, and controls, which for the longest time have been in the core of our system of education, will no longer exist as we have known them. This is true about curriculum, assessments, methodology, and, most importantly, learning environments.

Why is it so? Why is it that time-proven ways of schools carrying the sole responsibility for educating a next generation of human beings can no longer deliver the satisfactory outcome? Why cannot parents educate their children entirely on their own? To gain a better perspective, it is worth-while to take a quick look at the two worlds that many readers of this book have come to experience firsthand: the world of certainty and the world of uncertainty.

THE WORLD OF CERTAINTY AND THE
WORLD OF UNCERTAINTY

Education has always reflected and served the society. For the most of human history, learning was determined by necessities and was directly relevant to the lives that human beings led. For a long time, our world has been very pre-dictable. Over thousands of years, most human societies were self-contained, with not much interaction outside of their local communities. The traditional paradigm of education, as Yong Zhao (2012) calls it in his book, *World Class Learners*, which dominates virtually all schools in today's world, was reflective of our lives. Economically, the key for survival and prosperity alike was in maintaining order and preparing a labor force with similar skills and knowledge to support the local economy (p. 150).

In the third decade of the twentieth century, there have been a lot of changes in the United States. The world was shaken by war, with events in Europe and Asia hitting close to home. The automobile was altering patterns of urban and suburban lives and redefining distances and spaces. The Depression and unemployment affected many Americans. To improve and prosper, the local economy depended on a steady, reliable supply of workforce, making the questions of who should be trusted with such tasks and whether parents could live up to their responsibilities the hot topics of many debates.

Educators, social workers, and psychologists wrote at length about families and schools. More often than not, they told parents and teachers what they wanted to hear. Trust yourself, the experts said, because your judgment or instincts are right. But compared to the family, the school inspired greater confidence among those trained to dispense advice. More and more, pundits proclaimed, educators must take command. They should persuade families to have faith in schools. (Cutler III, 2000, p. 57)

Education of the masses required prescribed rote learning, based on a common curriculum, whereas mastery of content was a matter of survival. School and district leaders were held responsible for educational outcomes. There was a proven path that worked, led to success, and was seldom brought into question. In essence, this paradigm was a product of the evolution of our collective consciousness over many years of human history. Good jobs were realized and promotions were given based on a proven track record, a vision, clear ways to get there, and whether people followed the lead (Wheatley, 2000). Thus, our conceptualization of education was reflective of the times and made sense.

At the same time, relative isolation and homogeneity of human societies contributed to individual views and perceptions of personal happiness, which were often connected to a stable, comfortable, predictable, and controlled environment. It was safest to follow the same routines and find one's purpose in taking care of those around him or her. Deviations and differences were perceived by most individuals as undesirable, threatening, and needing correction.

Thus, the educational paradigm reflected this factor as well: Students knew how to get good grades, get into a good college, and earn a good stable job toward a comfortable future in their own community. Most tests were about knowing the right answer. Educators knew how to teach students to retain information. Schools were learning spaces and places with more learning places incorporated in individual classrooms. Teachers didn't have the need to heavily rely on parents or the community to affect learning.

For a few decades, this system worked. In the second half of the twentieth century, the United States was the global leader in education. It was the first country to implement, just like mass production, mass secondary education and there was noticeably an increase in college attendance. "As a result, the United States had the largest supply of highly qualified people in its adult labor force of any country in the world."

"This tremendous stock of highly educated human capital helped the United States to become the dominant economy in the world and to take advantage of the globalization and expansion of markets" (Stewart, 2012, p. 13). But it so happens that in the post-digital era, technology is deeply restructuring our society from how we used to know it, causing major shifts in three vital areas: job market and employment, global community and global issues, and formation of individual self, agency, and purpose.

Job Market and Employment

In the 1990s, advancements in communication networks caused a significant change to the U.S. job market by enabling computerized work to be relocated to low-wage countries. This affected many industries, including accounting, software development, and engineering design. Job creation and availability slowly decreased since 1980. As a result, the U.S. job market experienced a great dip. Nearly thirteen million members of the workforce lost their jobs from 2009 to 2011, followed by another 9.5 million members between 2011 and 2013. Those reemployed were not necessarily reemployed in the same industries from which they were displaced, according to the *Displaced Worker Summary Survey* produced by the U.S. Bureau of Labor Statistics (2014, August 26).

These data make it clear that the very nature of the work environment has changed, making it easier for new companies to be born, but more difficult for traditional companies to survive. This is the age, as Josh Linkner (2014) states in his book, *The Road to Reinvention*, "when nearly every industry is in the midst of massive upheaval . . . Dizzying speed, exponential complexity, and mind-numbing technology advances exacerbate the challenges we face as leaders" (p. 2).

In the story featuring five cases of personal and professional reinvention, published in *Fortune* magazine, Douglas Warshaw (2011, July 12) pinpoints one of the most uncomfortable consequence that the Third, Digital, Revolution has brought about—uncertainty. "The genesis of the piece was my realizing that just about everyone I know is sitting in their office—if they even have an office—spending no small part of their day thinking: 'How much longer is my job as I currently know it going to last? . . . And what the *blank* am I going to do next?'" (para. 1).

In the previous decade, freelancers started becoming a growing workforce. In 2015, there were nearly 54 million Americans freelancing, which was an increase of 700,000 over the previous year. That's more than a third of the U.S. workforce (Horowitz, 2015, October 2). The key for survival and prosperity in a project-based economy can no longer be in preparing a labor force with routine skills and knowledge; in fact, there is nothing routine about it at all: The most desirable freelance undertakings require skills and capacity to design, lead, and implement long-term projects with nonroutine deliverables.

Global Community and Global Issues

The world's social systems and cultures are quickly evolving. We constantly network with professionals from around the world; our children engage in playing games or sharing videos with youngsters across the ocean. The power of the global economy, the immediateness of global communications, and our ability to send and receive images and information have connected humankind in ways that are hard to fully comprehend. Nothing that occurs in one part of the world can remain hidden from another part of the world. In the era of digital communications, the concepts of privacy, connectedness, and community change.

Our immediate social environment has expanded radically, shifting from families, neighborhoods, and local communities to the entire world. This truly hits home when we realize that in a few decades, the Earth will most likely add another two billion people to its population, thus challenging nature's ability to sustain the planet.

> Humanity may soon be approaching the boundaries for global freshwater use, change in land use, ocean acidification and interference with the global phosphorous cycle. Our analysis suggests that three of the Earth-system processes—climate change, rate of biodiversity loss and interference with the nitrogen cycle—have already reached rates of change that cannot continue without significantly eroding the resilience of major components of Earth-system. (Rockström et al, 2009, p. 473)

Steve Cohen (2014, March 10), an executive director of Columbia University's Earth Institute, calls this issue of sustainability a distinctly global crisis, which often presents itself in different ways. Therefore, insights obtained in one area of the planet can be helpful in another. He suggests that knowledge on how to solve issues caused by West Virginia's chemical contamination of its drinking water, for example, might have lessons to offer to local governments in China.

> The transition to a sustainable economy will require the diffusion of new technologies and new modes of behavior. This will likely be accomplished across national boundaries, rather than within those boundaries. New technologies and new modes of behavior will be rapidly communicated and shared throughout the world. (para. 10)

In addition to the sustainability issue, microbiological threats will likely increase, as many human societies that have never or rarely come into contact with each other will increase their interactions and mix through major population movements. There is a real need to discover new practices. To keep up adequate living conditions, it is necessary to design new science, engineering, and architectural methods. Economic models to sustain their operations and maintenance are also a priority. No one nation can do this alone.

An Individual and Formation of Self, Agency, and Purpose

Since the 1960s, there has been an increasing agreement among economists on one key point: "the importance of people—their abilities, their knowledge, and their competences—to economic growth" (Keeley, 2007, p. 29). There has been a definite shift from mass production to personalization of products and services. The second decade of the twenty-first century also has a unique characteristic—a globalizing individual. There is a renewed emphasis on personal questions—questions about personal identity and how individuals, much more diverse, fit into the world.

Technology has provided numerous mobile applications (apps) that guide and advise us about everything—from how much sleep we get to detailed point-by-point directions to where we want to go. As the Internet and abundant social media gain ground, they affect individuals in both positive and negative ways. According to Howard Gardner and Katie Davis's book, *The App Generation* (2013):

> Apps can short-circuit identity formation, pushing you into being someone else's avatar [...] or, by foregrounding various options, they allow you to approach identity formation more deliberately, holistically, thoughtfully. You may end up with a stronger more powerful identity, or you may succumb to a prepackaged identity or to endless role diffusions. (p. 32)

The authors address the dual nature of technology influences on formation of self, noting that psychologists are concerned with youth's constant self-protection, self-polishing, and self-tracking online that take away time from quiet reflection and identity construction (pp. 74–76). Raised in the digital environment, as Ken Robinson (2014) points out, too many young people have no understanding of their true talents, lacking purpose in their lives. The overwhelming amount of evidence is everywhere: uninterested workers, alienated students, skyrocketing sales of antidepressants, and the number of suicides among our youth (p. xi).

One of the most impactful ways in which the digital era is altering self-identity is "through the shift from being internally to externally driven. Self-identity is no longer self-identity, meaning derived from the self, but rather is an identity projected onto us by popular culture and in no way an accurate reflection of who we really are" (Taylor, 2011, July 27, para. 7). Often, under this projected external polish hides profound fear, which is made known in an ongoing need for approval.

Invaded privacy, used publicly as a tool to humiliate a person, and a slipping sense of ownership reflect the moral and ethical dimensions of our interconnected lives and often shift a sense of agency away from the ethical dimensions. This is what Carrie James (2014) offers in her book, *Disconnected:* "*Blindspots* and *disconnects* are common to an unfortunate degree in mediated communication—when we interact, play, collaborate, and share content and ideas via text message, email, social media, and other virtual means" (p. 3).

Digital media can give the impression of closeness while promoting only shallow connections. Following Howard Gardner's (2012) differentiation of neighborly morality, involving concerns about those we know personally, and the ethics of roles, seen as a reflection of one's roles and associated responsibility, James (2014) separates self-interest, morality (dispositions of care and empathy), and ethics (impact on a wider community) in developing a sense of agency, stating that rarely modern youth are motivated by concerns of morality, and even less so by ethical considerations.

Thus, on the one hand, youth today exhibit "increasing eternalized, packed selves and a growing anxiety and aversion to risk-taking" (Gardner & Davis, 2013, p. 91). On the other hand, as there is much uncertainty in our future, the world needs a self-aware, adaptable, and ethical generation of human beings who are willing and capable of acting on issues beyond local significance. What does this mean for humankind? And what sets of skills and character traits are necessary for our youth to succeed in the world marked by the onset of the Fourth Industrial Revolution?

TWENTY-FIRST-CENTURY NEEDS

Today's workers have to know how to adapt, collaborate, think critically, communicate effectively, demonstrate initiative and entrepreneurialism, analyze and apply large amounts of information, and be curious. What also is emerging with renewed importance are agency, grit, empathy, and development of a global self.

4 C's

At the beginning of the twenty-first century, Guy Claxton (2002), a professor of education at Bristol, introduced 4 R's that are necessary for effective learning:

Resilience: "being ready, willing and able to lock on to learning." Being able
to stick with difficulty and cope with feelings such as fear and frustration.

Resourcefulness: "being ready, willing and able to learn in different ways."
Having a variety of learning strategies and knowing when to use them.

Reflection: "being ready, willing and able to become more strategic about learning." Getting to know our own strengths and weaknesses.

Relationships: "being ready, willing and able to learn alone and with others." (as
cited in Wegerif, 2010, p. 130)

These 4 R's parallel the 4 C's: critical thinking, communication, collaboration, and creativity. These are certainly the most needed skills for the global
future of today's youth. In a freelance economy, people change their professional identity frequently. To achieve true job security, one will have to stand
ready to reinvent oneself—no matter what age, education, skill set, or the
color of the collar (Warshaw, 2011, July 4, p. 70).

Over the past twenty to thirty years, "critical thinking" has become a hiring
requirement equivalent to a high school diploma at the least; everyone expects
it, but a high school diploma, or even a bachelor's degree, doesn't guarantee
it. "Students might use words and ideas, but do not know how to think ideas
through, and internalize foundational meanings. They take classes but cannot
make connections between the logic of a discipline and what is important in
life" (How to study and learn, part. 1, 2013, para. 1). Thinking is a bridge that
connects existing knowledge to what it could become in the real world.

The twenty-first century calls for creative thinkers who can recognize
opportunities and have inclinations to respond to them. The world is changing very rapidly. By the time someone graduates, a lot of the knowledge he
or she acquired may already be outdated. "The main thing that students need
to know is not what to think but how to think in order to face new challenges
and solve new problems" (Lang, 2012, p. 14).

There is also a need for "thinking-centered values, commitments, sen-
sitivities and belief systems, in addition to thinking skills" (Tishman &
Palmer, 2007, pp. 90–91). Good thinking consists of abilities, attitudes,
and alertness—all three at once. Schools need to offer students educational
experiences that will help them learn to identify their own challenges, solve
problems, develop creativity in thinking, work together, inspire others, and
share their knowledge.

Agency and Character Traits

The reality that students from all over the world will be competing with
U.S. students for many jobs calls for specific character traits. "As our fast-
paced world could unexpectedly throw anyone off a familiar path, the reason

some people become successful is more about attitude than knowledge of facts" (Warshaw, 2011, July 4, p. 70). In real life, problems rarely come precisely wrapped and easily understood, making perseverance and a growth mindset key characteristics of success and achievement. Students have to possess academic knowledge and know how to read, write, and multiply, but this is only a start. Children have to develop a belief that they can be in charge of their own lives no matter in what circumstances they might find themselves in the future.

A list of qualities of high-achieving people has always likely included self-efficacy, self-confidence, and grit, but now they matter more than ever before. In the study conducted along with Christopher Peterson, Michael Matthews, and Dennis Kelly, Angela Duckworth (2007) defined *grit* as "working strenuously toward challenges, maintaining effort and interest over years despite failure, adversity, and plateaus in progress" (p. 1088).

When disappointment or failure makes many people change trajectory and cut losses, the gritty individual stays the course. Across six studies, individual differences in grit accounted for significant variance in success outcomes over and beyond that explained by IQ, to which it was not positively related. Psychologists note the significance of one's belief in one's own ability to affect change, or as sociologists Jan Stets and Peter Burke (2000) describe it, "seeing oneself as a causal agent in one's life" (p. 32), in success and achievement. A developed sense of agency serves as a foundation for many other essential skills, allowing individuals to take control of their lives.

A sense of purpose—how "what I know and do" enables me to make a difference—largely rests on two major beliefs: a belief in one's own capacity to, loosely put, accumulate knowledge, and a belief in one's own ability to productively apply this knowledge to reach a desired end. In other words, it's a combination of information, its application, and consequential satisfaction of seeing that this makes a difference. A direction that brings the most satisfaction, however, is often hard to establish, as a key to it is in discovery of one's own power.

Further, an understanding of how one's actions may affect other people is an essential component to living in human society. Sensitivity to perspectives and feelings of others and moral considerations are necessary to form successful relationships of any kind. Even technical businesses are starting to believe that they first need to understand the customer's inner experience and personal vantage point. "Designing emotion into the product is now something you really have to think about explicitly and measure yourself against," says Brad Smith, CEO of Intuit (as cited in Colvin, 2014, September 4, para. 1). As a result, companies are looking for something previously inconsequential in their new employees: empathy.

On the contrary, considerable evidence suggests that, nowadays, young people are less empathetic than youth in the 1980s and 1990s (Konrath et al, 2011). A recent survey of 10,000 middle- and high school students, published by the Harvard Graduate School of Education's Making Caring Common Project, has found that caring for others isn't a top priority.

"When asked to rank what was most important to them—achieving at a high level, happiness, or caring for others—almost 80 percent of the surveyed students chose high achievement or happiness as their top choice, while only 20 percent chose caring for others" (Hough, 2014, September 8, para. 2). In his analysis of seventh- and eighth-grade fiction, Howard Gardner (Gardner & Davis, 2013) identified a decrease over a decade in a number of stories in which a character, featured by an author, was rather different from the author himself or herself: 32% in the mid-1990s versus 0% in the late 2000s (p. 111).

Global Citizenship

As a part of understanding one's own self, living in the twenty-first century requires the development of one's global self: "identity and sense of belonging to see ourselves as participating actors in a rich global matrix. As we come into contact with new people, ideas, products or situations; as we take note of these experiences and seek to understand, we also deepen our understanding of ourselves and our role in this world of ours" (Boix Mansilla, 2013, September 15, para. 3).

In 2002, the UNESCO Prize for Peace Education was awarded to the City Montessori School in India "in recognition of its efforts to promote the universal values of education for peace and tolerance and to renew the principles of secularism at a time when these values and principles are increasingly being challenged" (UNESCO, 2002, June 6). The school was founded on four essential principles: universal values, excellence, global understanding, and service to the community. Its students consistently scored higher on exams than the national average. More importantly, for more than 40 years, it had educated students to respect the values of tolerance and peace.

Harvard Professor Fernando Reimers (2009) sees developing positive dispositions toward cultural differences (an interest and understanding of different civilizational streams and the ability to see them as opportunities for constructive transactions among people) as a must to create tolerance. Children need knowledge and flexible, adaptive tools to become successful in an interconnected society and to develop an acceptance of differences. As a preparation to live in a global environment, students need "knowledge of foreign languages and cultures to market products to customers around the globe and to work effectively with foreign employees and partners in other countries" (The Research & Policy Committee of the Committee for Economic Development, 2006, pp. 1, 2).

There is a slowly growing trend of U.S. students studying abroad and foreign students studying in the United States. The number of Americans studying abroad grew by 7.2% in 2012–13 to an all-time high of 819,644, based on the "Open Doors" survey of international enrollments and the U.S. study abroad participation. When "undertaken correctly, these programs can build understanding and empathy" (Cohen 2014, March 10, para. 5). Throughout all of this, young people can collaborate with each other, as well as virtually with students across the globe, and develop problem-solving and cross-cultural communication skills that are necessary for a global marketplace.

As these needs emerge, those in charge of public education surely must realize that to provide the new generation of Americans with what will be required from it in just a few years, schools need to change. And since ways of living have changed drastically, then schools, too, should have begun a journey toward nurturing self-motivated learners, who are able to generate and apply knowledge in multiple ways. However, "there is evidence that current educational policies do in fact have an inhibiting role when it comes to opening up learning, promoting creativity, and promoting thinking" (Ritchhart, 2015, p. 26).

EDUCATION

For the past 30 years, many nations have been expanding education to improve individual well-being and economic growth. Asia has been moving ahead with lightning speed, given the expansion of the middle class in India and China, along with rapidly expanding secondary and higher education systems. As a result, the United States no longer produces the most educated workforce.

"While *older* generations of Americans are better educated than their international peers, many other countries have a higher proportion of *younger* workers with completed college degrees" (Stewart, 2012, p. 15). Because education of its population is seen as an indicator of a country's economic stability and growth, the high school diploma became the norm throughout the globe. That set forth the questions of which nation did best educating its youth and how teenagers in one country could be compared with their counterparts in another. Thus, international comparisons in education were born.

Common Sense Behind Testing

In the United States, citizens hear a lot about failing schools and international test scores that don't favor U.S. youth. Back in 1983, the National Commission on Education released *A Nation at Risk* report, stating that the educational foundations of the society were "being eroded by a rising tide of mediocrity." This statement was based on the following indicators:

- International comparisons of student achievement revealed that on 19 academic tests U.S. students were never first or second and, in comparison with other industrialized nations, were last seven times.
- Some 23 million U.S. adults were functionally illiterate by the simplest tests of everyday reading, writing, and comprehension.
- About 13% of all 17-year-olds in the United States were functionally illiterate.
- Average achievement of high school students on most standardized tests had decreased in the previous 26 years.
- More than half the population of gifted students did not match their tested ability with comparable achievements in school.
- The SAT [Scholastic Assessment Test] demonstrated a decline with average verbal scores, average mathematics scores, and scores in physics and English, and the number of students demonstrating superior achievement on the SATs also decreased.
- Many 17-year-olds did not possess the "higher order" intellectual skills, such as drawing inferences from written material, writing a persuasive essay, or solving a mathematics problem requiring several steps.
- There was a steady decline in science achievement scores of the United States.
- Remedial mathematics courses in public four-year colleges increased by 72%.
- Average tested achievement of students graduating from college was also lower.
- Business and military leaders spent millions of dollars on costly remedial education and training programs in basic skills such as reading, writing, spelling, and computation (United States, 1983).

Test results were not the sole criterion for the alarm, but they certainly did play a major role. The intent behind this report was very commendable: "to develop the talents of all to their fullest. Attaining that goal requires that we expect and assist all students to work to the limits of their capabilities. We should expect schools to have genuinely high standards rather than minimum ones, and parents to support and encourage their children to make the most of their talents and abilities" (United States, 1983). The committee recommended a stronger curriculum, higher graduation requirements, more homework, longer school hours, and testing to measure the progress.

However, when 30 years later, in December of 2013, Secretary of Education Arne Duncan released the results of the latest international assessment of student performance (PISA) in reading, science, and mathematics, Shanghai led the nations of the world in all three categories; whereas U.S. students, again, were not up to the par compared with students in 61 other countries. If the previous measures didn't seem to work, what could be the problem? Was it the issue of inadequate education that was not doing its job in preparing the next generation of Americans for a successful, fulfilling life or was it the issue of the tests failing to truly reflect an individual's "life-worthy" (Perkins, 2014) knowledge and skills?

It seemed to be a vicious circle. On the one hand, used as a quality control, tests themselves couldn't fully measure the quality of the human mind or accurately assess high-order thinking. According to Diane Ravitch (2014, November 20), Americans never did well on the international tests. On the first such test in mathematics, in 1964, U.S. high school seniors scored the last among 12 nations, and eighth-grade students scored next to last. "Nonetheless, in the following fifty years, the U.S. outperformed the other eleven nations by every measure, whether economic productivity, military might, technological innovation, or democratic institutions" (para. 11).

On the other hand, when tests become high stake and are viewed as learning outcomes rather than tools, there is a real possibility that schools would be transformed from places of learning into test drilling factories. This, in turn, would negatively affect learning. Yong Zhao's *Who's Afraid of the Big Bad Dragon?* (2009) offers some insight toward maintaining economic growth. China needs technological innovation, which can only be achieved if it abandons its test-based education system. China's claim of the best education system is based on its success in producing the highest test scores, but the pursuit of these scores costs Chinese students their creativity and ability for unconventional thinking.

In addition, provided that the lion's share of test preparations happens in after-school tutoring establishments, school systems in China cannot rightfully claim the responsibility for the scores. Zhao (2009) also suggests that China's outstanding economic growth has nothing to do with its education system, but with opening its markets to foreign investments, utilizing Western technology, and allowing students to attend colleges in Western institutions. The more China moves away from central planning, the better its economy is. Two major forces that are used to restructure China's education system, Zhao believes, are globalization and technology.

Every Student Doesn't Succeed

In 1994, the U.S. Congress passed *Goals 2000: Educate America Act of 1993—* President Clinton's program—which targeted, among other goals, that by the year 2000, U.S. students would be first in the world in mathematics and science and all children would start school ready to learn. It also awarded money to states for creating their own standards and tests to make sure that the goals were met.

As the nation did not meet these goals, in 2002, President George W. Bush came up with his own program to fix the U.S. education system: *No Child Left Behind* (NCLB). It ordered states to annually test every student in grades three through eight in reading and mathematics and mandated that all children become proficient in these subjects by 2014. Schools that did not show sufficient improvement toward the goal could become subjects for forced closure, state takeover, or handing over to private management (No Child Left Behind [NCLB], 2002). It seems plausible that with the passage of NCLB, fearing closure and the loss of jobs, many schools could have become more concerned with teaching to the test than with student learning.

Ten years later, the Obama administration changed the tactics: Instead of the punitive measures, *Race to the Top* encouraged states to compete for some $4.35 billion in federal funds if they promoted privately managed charter schools, reformed their low-performing schools, and evaluated teachers largely based on the test scores of their students. Adoption of rigorous standards, including the Common Core, was another requirement to ensure that students were leaving schools college and career ready (*Race to the Top Act of 2011*, 2012).

The *Every Student Succeeds Act* (ESSA), signed by President Obama on December 10, 2015, was greeted by many with a long-awaited relief. Most notably, the new law didn't require states to evaluate teachers based in any substantial degree on students' test scores. However, annual standardized tests were still expected to measure the learning of those who live in a largely unstandardized world. Students in grades three to eight will be tested annually and at least once in high school, and the scores will still impact school evaluations. In addition, the decision what rewards or sanctions will follow is left up to states (*Every Student Succeeds Act of 2015*). There is no guarantee that all of the states have the capacity to develop anything noticeably better than what they used in the previous decade.

It seems rather obvious: On its own, testing every child once a year does not accurately reflect an individual's progress nor does it lead to every child's success. There are children who perform well on these tests, but whose growth is capped below their individual abilities. There are children who might not perform well for various reasons, but who experience substantial individual growth as learners.

If this test-based education system, credited for the high performance of Shanghai, Hong Kong, and East Asian nations on the international tests, doesn't produce a learning environment that promotes the development of dispositions for critical thinking, creativity, and adaptability and is going to prevent these nations from fully developing their economic potential, why does the United States want to outperform them? And if the United States wishes to show better results, are there better ways to get there?

In the recent past, there have been a number of transformational theories through the lens of the world's education systems and their appropriateness in our social context (Kozol, 2005; Abbot, 2010; Stewart, 2012; Zhao, 2009; 2012; Ravitch, 2013). Educational, neuroscience, and psychological research has brought into focus new ways of learning, engendering myriad innovative educational theories, concepts, frameworks, and understandings toward better teaching and learning, including: big understandings (Perkins, 2014), cultures of thinking (Ritchhart, 2015), visible thinking (Ritchhart, Church, & Morrison, 2011), brain-based learning (Jensen, 2008), emotion and learning (Immordino-Yang, 2011), the Maker Movement, project-based learning (Martinez & Stager, 2013), the Community of Inquiry (Akyol & Garrison, 2013), blended learning (Horn & Staker, 2014), and learner-centered teaching (Doyle, 2011), to name just a few of them.

As our world is changing, affecting the areas of employment, community, and individuals, educational thought leaders conceptualize new approaches and mindsets that respond to demands of the new times. One of the top priorities among them is understanding and influencing learning environments that surround a learner throughout his or her life. The concept of a learning environment, explored from the perspective of various tiers that together create a comprehensive matrix of factors and players that affect a child's learning, is the focus of chapter 2.

Chapter 1 Snapshot: THE FOURTH INDUSTRIAL REVOLUTION AND ITS IMPACT ON EDUCATION

FOCUS AREA	TRENDS	NEEDS
Market and Employment	Project-based economy and global competition	Dispositions for critical thinking, communication, collaboration, and creativity Adaptability and flexibility
Global Community and Global Issues	Changing nature of privacy, connectedness, community Issues of sustainability and microbiological threats	Development of a global self

(continued)

Chapter 1 Snapshot (*continued*)

FOCUS AREA	TRENDS	NEEDS
An Individual and Formation of Self, Agency, and Purpose	Personalization—a renewed emphasis on an individual Questions about the personal identity and how individuals fit into the world Influence of technology on the formation of self	Developed sense of agency, self-efficacy, and grit Empathy—sensitivity to perspectives and feelings of others Moral and ethical considerations—responsibility to others and a larger community
Education	A shift from: Rote learning to real learning Memorization to high-order thinking Tests only to comprehensive assessment systems Accumulation of knowledge to application of knowledge Subject segregation to interdisciplinary and blended learning	Developing in students dispositions for critical thinking, communication, collaboration, and creativity Nurturing a positive disposition toward cultural differences and a disposition to act on global issues Developing student agency and providing opportunities for social and emotional learning

Canvas for Learning

"Powerful learning environment will be creating synergies and finding new ways to enhance professional and cultural capital of others. They will do this with families and communities, higher education, businesses..."

—OECD

At its very basic definition, the term *learning environment* implies a combination of two distinctly important and complex concepts: *an environment* and *learning*. An individual exists surrounded by many environments—from a family environment, to a work environment, to a cultural environment, to a global environment. Any environment has a set of various attributes, namely how it looks (visual appeal), feels (physical, cultural, social, and emotional characteristics), and supports the needs of people (resources) who are expected to perform various tasks in its setting. An environment also has a function that becomes a driving force behind its creation and existence. When it comes to a learning environment, the main function of this environment is to promote, facilitate, and ignite learning.

A *learning environment* is not a new term. The concept of a *learning space*, which originally referred to a specific location where learning took place, has been at the heart of the educational enterprise for many years. There is a need, however, for terms and concepts defined by learning, not the formal institutional system of schooling. Thus, a new set of questions is necessary for this conversation:

- What is learning?
- What factors influence learning?

- What are the components of a learning environment?
- How do multiple learning environments connect into a larger learning environment?
- How do the roles and responsibilities of an educator, a learner, a parent, and a local and distant community member evolve as the society moves toward larger learning environments?
- What culture within educational systems promotes nurturing, productive larger learning environments?
- How do we build such a culture?

WHAT IS LEARNING?

Individual variations in learning are usually results of two main influences: nature and nurture. The former refers to differences in a biological makeup of human beings: their genetics. The latter is determined by the distinctiveness of each person's physical, social, emotional, and cultural environments. In every classroom, students differ in many ways that are essential to their learning: "prior knowledge, ability, conceptions of learning, learning styles and strategies, interest, motivation, self-efficacy beliefs and emotion; they differ also in socio-environmental terms such as linguistic, cultural and social backgrounds" (Dumont, Istance, & Benavides, 2010, p. 4). There is always a dynamic relationship between nurture and nature in learning.

Nature and Learning

For a long time, there seemed to be a widely accepted belief that children are born either smart or not so smart. Often, formal education began with this preconception that biology determined the intellectual characteristics with which children were born; they were fixed and unfolded independent of experience. Children's social and cultural experiences, including their schooling, only reflected these biological predispositions and couldn't be influenced (Immordino-Yang & Fisher, 2010, p. 310). Thus, some children were seen as more intelligent than others; some children could learn and some couldn't. This mindset affected how educators approached student learning, and, therefore, understood and constructed a learning environment.

Research in neuroplasticity and neurobiology, however, has shown that the human brain is pliable, plastic, and improvable. It is constantly being shaped and re-shaped through interaction with the environment (Williamson, 2014, December 8). What this means is that children's experiences shape their biology as much as biology shapes children's development. Learning involves actively constructing neural networks that connect many brain areas.

"Due to the constructive nature of this process, different learners' networks may differ, in accordance with the person's neuropsychological strengths and predispositions, and with the cultural, physical, and social context in which the skills are built" (Immordino-Yang & Fisher, 2010, p. 312). Therefore, it is the environment that either promotes or stumbles learning.

Moreover, intelligence is a rather complex concept. Howard Gardner (1995) theorized the idea of multiple intelligences based on the extent to which learners have various types of minds and, as a result, remember and process information in different ways:

> We are all able to know the world through language, logical-mathematical analysis, spatial representation, musical thinking, the use of the body to solve problems or to make things, an understanding of other individuals, and an understanding of ourselves. Where individuals differ is in the strength of these intelligences and in the ways in which such intelligences are invoked and combined to carry out different tasks, solve diverse problems, and progress in various domains. (p. 12)

Gardner (1999) insists that individuals are not equally smart in all circumstances; instead, they have different intelligences, which are activated by what is valued as a person's ability to solve problems or to create products at a particular historical time in a particular cultural context. Thus, if all human beings are capable of learning but learn in different ways, a learning environment should provide what is necessary for all types of learners.

Developments in neuroscience have also established a scientific base for what many intuitive teachers have known for ages: Learning is much more complex than works of one area of the brain. Educators often focus on neural networks for domain-specific skills such as reading and math, whereas domain-general and emotion-related networks function as modulators and facilitators of memory and domain-specific learning. These networks include emotion, social processing, and attention (Immordino-Yang & Fisher, 2010, p. 313). Given that schools are educating young children, this raises a whole different set of questions regarding a learning environment.

An emotionally appealing environment, its characteristics conductive to learning, and how to foster it within schools and classrooms have been addressed by many educators, simultaneously re-thinking learning physical space. Since different students are the most comfortable in different settings, many classrooms now provide alternative spaces. Some spaces feature cushions and comfortable seating areas to read and to do work either individually or with peers. Some educators create innovative spaces to reflect and value each child's specific interests and strengths by offering choices and learning activities that are appropriate for various learners.

Formal and informal learning environments are also being reconsidered. Schools have been rapidly expanding curricula, placing children in a formal educational setting earlier, and giving extensive homework in hopes of improving their achievement. Back in the eighteenth century, however, Jean-Jacques Rousseau (1979) advised that formal education should not be started until adolescence, and children, like small animals, should be freed of constrictive, swaddling clothes and allowed to play outside, thereby developing their physical senses, which become the most important tools in their acquisition of knowledge.

Supported by a number of anthropological, psychological, neuroscientific, and educational studies, Cambridge researcher David Whitebread (2014, September 24) urged the UK government "in the interest of children's academic achievements and their emotional well-being" to take evidence regarding negative effects of "too much too soon" seriously (para. 1). This evidence included the following:

- Neuroscientific studies linked play to synaptic growth in the frontal cortex of the brain, which is responsible for all human higher mental functions.
- Developmental psychology studies demonstrated the superior learning and motivation arising in playful settings, as opposed to instructional settings.
- Some of the studies compared groups of children in New Zealand who started formal literacy lessons at ages 5 and 7. The results showed that not only did the early introduction of formal learning approaches to literacy not improve children's reading development but also, potentially, it was damaging. (paras. 3–5)

Information and assignment overload, which often accompanies mastering the content through repetition and redundant practices, also raises some questions about learning. "Nearly four in ten parents (38%) with children in grades 9-12, and over a third (36%) of parents of children in grades 6-8 say their child experienced a lot of stress," reveals a poll conducted by NPR (National Public Radio), the Robert Wood Johnson Foundation, and the Harvard School of Public Health (2013, September, p. 9).

Mary Alvord, a clinical psychologist in Maryland and a public education coordinator for the American Psychological Association (APA), states that chronic stress causes a sense of panic and paralysis: "The child feels stuck, which only adds to the feeling of stress" (as cited in Neighmond, 2013, December 2, para. 10).

An environment where children feel valued and encouraged to take risks and experiment with something new is where learning happens. Would it be plausible, then, to suggest that if educators create an accepting, collaborative, and appealing-to-all-learners physical space that also promotes self-management and developing adaptive skills, every child will learn?

The key to this answer is in an obvious but consequential fact that student learning is not something that can be achieved by teachers or school administrators. It can only happen within an individual human being. Human consciousness, passions, values, and thought—exactly what makes up human beings—are all important parts of learning, and they expand much beyond an individual classroom.

Nurture and Learning

There is nothing more complex than a human being and his or her mysterious engine, the human brain. As the world has changed over thousands of years, the way people experience it remains the same: "through the single lens of the *self*" (Rock & Bokas, 2015, March 7). And this self is as unique as a set of fingerprints. Since the "What am I?" thought first entered the human mind at the dawn of civilization, human beings have been in a constant search for self-identity.

René Descartes' (1639) sophisticated argument that the individual self was the first thing each individual could know for certain defined the mind, or self-consciousness, as the essence of self-identity. Thinking was the key: "I think; therefore, I am." John Locke (1839), the English philosopher, proposed that the self was not the whole of consciousness but just a specific part of the mind: our memory containing the past. This explains why an individual thinks of himself or herself as the same person over time, even though there may have been drastic changes. "The identity of the same man consists in nothing but a participation of the same continued life, by constantly fleeting particles of matter, in succession vitally united to the same organized body" (p. 223).

Other aspects of consciousness may also define the self. Søren Kierkegaard (2009), from Dania, believed that one's most important mission in life was to cultivate the self by cultivating one's passions. In his *Unscientific Postscript* (1846), he defined the self in terms of passions, concluding that it was impossible to exist without passion, unless we understood the word *exist* in the loose sense as *existence*.

A modern debate about the emotions started with philosopher–psychologist William James. In his essay "What Is an Emotion?" James (1884) argued that emotions were feelings, but a very specific kind of feelings. They were the feelings caused by changes in the body from upsetting perceptions. "The bodily changes follow directly the PERCEPTION of the existing fact and our feeling of the same changes as they occur" (pp. 189–190). Self-consciousness was determined by what emotions were the most prevalent and how they got expressed. Thus, who we are depends on how we feel about things.

At the same time, the image that individuals have of themselves is significantly influenced by what they have been taught collectively by the society, exactly because people are more than individuals. According to Jim Taylor (2011, July 27), people gain self-identities in two ways: self-awareness and feedback from a social world. Self-awareness comes from observing one's own thoughts, emotions, and actions based on prior experiences, immediate needs, and future aspirations.

Humans also look outward to their environment for feedback that, too, shapes their self-identities. "Because we are fundamentally social beings and an essential part of our development involves finding our place in the social and cultural context in which we live, feedback from that social world plays a significant role in the evolution of our self-identities" (para. 2), which happens through ongoing learning.

There is much to be said about humankind's philosophical pursuits, concepts, and theories about its own existence and learning, but it appears that there has been one general trend—an oversimplification, a one-answer-only approach, and a separation more frequent than integration. However, just as the human brain is an extremely complex and interconnected organism, everything else empowered by it is also as complex and interconnected. A human being is a combination of self and others, individual and collective, one's own purposes and benefits to all. One's own self is a combination of memory, thinking, rationality, aesthetics, passion, desire, will, values, and emotions. None of these could be dismissed.

This leads to one important understanding: Children do not learn in isolation, but they develop physically, socially, emotionally, ethically, and intellectually within their families, schools, neighborhoods, and communities (ASCD, 2007, p. 11). Today, "the dominant concept [of learning] is *socioconstructivist* in which learning is understood to be importantly shaped by the context in which it is *situated* and is *actively constructed* through *social negotiation* with others" (Dumont et al, 2010, p. 3). What students experience in their lives outside of a classroom, their circumstances, might either enable their learning or undermine their ability to learn and progress in school. For children growing in chronic poverty or victims of domestic violence, for example, daily survival often becomes the main goal, as their well-being is threatened by something out of their control.

According to the National Center on Family Homelessness, based on the definition of homelessness that schools are required to use under the federal McKinney-Vento Act, in 2012–13, one out of every 30 children in the United States experienced homelessness at some point during the year, which made this nearly 2.5 million children, up from 1.6 million in 2010. These children usually have considerable developmental problems and mental health needs (Khadaroo, 2014, November 17). Many communities across the nation face staggering socioeconomic costs resulting from the growing numbers of children and youth with "highly complex barriers to learning" (Kochhar-Bryant, 1997, p. 2).

The Association for Supervision and Curriculum Development (ASCD, 2007) delineated six out-of-school factors, commonly present among the poor, that impact students' learning opportunities and make schools unable to advance them on their own: low birth weight and nongenetic prenatal influences on children; inadequate medical, dental, and vision care; food insecurity; environmental pollutants; family relations and stress; and neighborhood characteristics.

As important as these factors are in affecting learning of many students, setting low expectations of disadvantaged students doesn't serve them well. "The first 20 years of digital learning suggest that most human beings learn and grow in relationship" (Vander Ark, 2016, February 17, para. 4); thus, influence of teachers is also one of the most important factors in how much students are motivated to learn. Expecting the most out of students and disregarding common assumptions about the limits of students' abilities based on their socioeconomic or racial factors can have a dramatic positive impact.

> Students tend to believe and respect the evaluations that teachers make of them. Thus, if the teacher publicly commends a low status student for being strong on a particular (and real) ability, that student will tend to believe the evaluation. At the same time, the other students in the classroom are likely to accept the evaluation as valid. Once this happens, the expectations for the student's competence—as well as his/her relative status in the classroom—can rise dramatically, which is likely to result in increased activity and influence of the low status student as well as increased success in future classroom tasks. (Quintero, 2014, April 30, para. 17)

Ronald Ferguson (2002), an economist and a researcher at Harvard University, conducted a survey of more than 30,000 Black, White, Hispanic, Asian, and mixed-race students. "One of the most interesting results of this study is the distinctive importance of teacher encouragement as a source of motivation for non-White students" (p. 25). Ferguson concluded that an "increase in effort is unlikely to occur without approaches to instruction that push students toward higher goals and make achieving those goals both feasible and rewarding" (2002, p. 15).

Learning results from "the dynamic interplay of emotion, motivation and cognition, and these are inextricably intertwined" (Dumont et al, 2010, p. 6). Although schools and teachers play a significant part in shaping student learning, it is affected by wider influences than those that can be controlled by the educational enterprise within a learning environment of an educational establishment. And the unfortunate truth is that schools alone cannot provide sufficient supporting environments for all students.

ASCD (2007) is calling for a change that can have far-reaching impacts: "put the child at the center of decision making and allocate resources—time, space, and human—to ensure each child's success. We call for a shift in how schools and communities look at young people's learning. Lay aside the perennial battles for resources and instead align those resources in support of the whole child" (p. 19). This makes it necessary to re-think the concept of a learning environment in its entirety.

LEARNING ENVIRONMENTS

A *learning environment* traditionally referred to a place, often within the walls of an educational institution, such as a classroom or a library, where students were expected to learn. Of course, there is a lot of learning that happens in these places, but the dynamics of our times and new discoveries in neuroscience about what happens in the human brain when it learns significantly shift the scope of environmental factors that influence learning.

Learning is not limited to the walls of a classroom or school. Often, it happens in places and spaces that people don't associate with learning. It can occur at a family dinner table, community or sport event, or movie theater—every place or surrounding where a child spends time presents opportunities for learning. Moreover, in today's interconnected and technology-driven world, a learning environment can be nowhere—virtual—which means that it might not have a physical place.

21st Century Education suggests that a more accurate way to think of twenty-first-century learning environments is as of "the support systems" that organize the condition in which children learn. "Learning environments are the structures, tools, and communities that inspire students and educators to attain the knowledge and skills the twenty-first century demands of us all" (Partnership for 21st Century Skills, n.d.). A learning environment is a combination of diverse physical locations, contexts, and cultures in which students learn (Bates, 2015), starting perhaps with a physical or virtual space and covering, more broadly, a set of principles that educators incorporate into a conventional space-influenced model.

Thus, the term *learning environment* denotes the totality of the surroundings and conditions in which someone learns, and it consists of a wide set of features that affect individual learning. As our world is on the threshold of the new interconnectedness that erases physical, digital, and biological spheres, a learning environment can no longer be defined by a school location. The only limitations that humankind still has, and probably not for long, are the limitations of its own physical domain called the planet Earth. This is the space where learning happens.

Provided that within this space there are thousands of biological, cultural, religious, and socioeconomic variations (not counting soon to be 8.2 billion of individually learning brains), the task of shaping a learning environment of an individual learner seems like an impossible endeavor. However, the Fourth Industrial Revolution is brought about by fusion that is also blurring the lines of what were traditionally seen as prerogatives of educational systems, making educational boundaries and isolation not only extremely limiting but also nearly impossible.

Micro Level and Macro Level

Recognizing that isolation within a world of complex learning systems seriously limits potential, the report from the Organization for Economic Co-Operation Development (OECD, 2015) *Innovative Learning Environments* project brought forward the concept of learning ecosystems: "interdependent combinations of different species of providers and organizations playing different roles with learners in different relationships to them over time and varying mixes" (p. 13). The report delineates three levels:

- The "learning environment" or micro level as referring to a location where learning takes place
- The "meso" level as comprising the many compounds of the learning environment in networks, communities, chains, and initiatives, which is vital for sustaining innovative learning
- The "meta" level as the aggregation of all the learning environments and connections that come within the chosen boundaries (p. 13)

When considering a learning environment, it is necessary to look at it from a perspective of multiple tiers. In practice, it might mean that there is a learning environment that is created and sustained within an individual classroom, or a bit larger, an individual school. Then, there are learning environments that emerge when this school's learning environment overlaps or connects with other learning environments outside of this school's location. Even though there are multiple components to each one, it is possible to differentiate between two distinct levels of a learning environment—a micro learning environment and a macro learning environment.

A micro learning environment refers to a physically contained space, such as a classroom or home, that is created and maintained by the internal forces of this environment's providers. There has been a lot of research and accumulated knowledge on how to build such environments at schools, where teachers, administrators, and students collaborate and learn together.

These environments are created based on a school's or district's learning values and beliefs, understanding of learning differences and needs of learners, smart use and innovative arrangement of physical spaces, and the attention to an emotional and physical security of learners. In other words, at this level, the focus is on creating an appealing secure place where all types of learners will feel safe, challenged, and valued.

In addition, provided that an individual's perception of self is gained through a direct experience with environments and is influenced by others, what educators deem to be valuable and true largely translates into how students see themselves as learners and people. Therefore, it's essential to pay attention to what is highlighted as important at school. A positive learning environment is based on the values of trust, kindness, and acceptance. If they think about and respect the feelings of others, children can collaborate much better due to their willingness to listen for understanding.

Students should also be encouraged to challenge themselves, grow as learners, and develop a growth mindset. A focus on developing thinking provides greater engagement, deeper understanding of content as well as shapes learners' attitudes toward thinking and learning. Eventually, it leads to a community of eagerly engaged thinkers who are capable of taking responsibility for their own learning.

Apart from standards set in classrooms, however, learning is affected by standards drawn from home, the workplace, and the community. "Students view not only teachers, but also family members and mentors as allies in their achievement" (Washor, 2014, November 17, para. 5). This brings the concept of a learning environment to a macro level.

A macro learning environment refers to the entire context of influences that come from all of the learning environments that a child enters. Some learning environments will overlap with the environment of the classroom (such as an online learning environment facilitated by the use of technology), and some will come into close contact with it. *Schooling Re-designed: Towards Innovative Learning Systems* (OECD, 2015) report claims that a powerful learning environment should be in a constant process of creating synergies and seeking new ways to improve professional, social, and cultural capital of others, especially with family and communities, businesses, educational establishments, and other learning environments (p. 19).

In other words, a micro learning environment can be truly powerful only when it connects to and becomes part of a bigger environmental canvas at a macro level—when it constantly interacts with other environments that affect learning, influencing them and evolving with them.

Shifting Responsibilities

Schools, Families, and Communities as Creators of Learning Environments

In a traditional micro learning environment, the responsibility for creating an atmosphere that is conductive to student learning usually falls on teachers and administrators. It is school and district leaders' responsibility to provide students with a physical space that is safe, comfortable, and responsive to students' physical and learning needs. It is the responsibility of a teacher to arrange space so that all learners' needs are met, create and enforce rules that eliminate disruption, and model behaviors that promote thinking and learning. Many educators do see their goal in helping learners grow into accomplished, independently thinking individuals who are capable of leaving a lasting impression on the world.

Then, there are other micro environments that directly affect student learning: learning environments at home and surrounding community places where children physically spend time. It seems logical that parents and family members are responsible for a learning environment at home; whereas community organizations, agencies, clubs, studios, and sport establishments are responsible for learning environments within their physical spaces.

This responsibility is less clear when it comes to online learning environments that don't have a physical space. Often, people look to companies providing various online activities to act as guarantors of positive learning environments. This, however, doesn't always happen, shifting the responsibility back to teachers, parents, or most likely, learners themselves. This makes it very clear: Learners themselves are an integral part of any learning environment they enter. As learners shift between various environments, including those in virtual spaces, they affect these environments and others in these environments, just as these environments affect them.

How well students can develop as learners within a classroom learning environment depends on synergies with other learning environments that every child enters. If a learning environment at school is similar to one at home, there are no contradicting messages to interfere with the process of learning. On the other hand, if at school a teacher strives for an environment that promotes curiosity and thinking, but at home, a student's thinking is not valued and the focus is placed on adult authority, it might create confusion for a learner in both learning environments.

Similarly, if a classroom environment de-emphasizes outcomes and focuses on the learning process and collaboration, but a sport-related environment emphasizes winning, competition, and results, a child might be affected by the dissonance. School memories of most adults are of the educational system that promotes compliance and competition: What needs to be learned is given by the teacher who also makes arbitrary decisions about the right and wrong answers (Madrazo & Senge, 2011, p. 5). This often leads to home and community learning environments that are based on these beliefs.

Learners as Creators of Their Learning Environment

The foundations of sound mental health are built early in life, and early experiences, including children's relationships with families, teachers, and peers, are vital in the formation of self-motivation in learning. "Disruptions in this developmental process can impair a child's capacities for learning and relating to others, with lifelong implications" (Center on the Developing Child, n.d.). Most children learn to assimilate into what is valued in each environment, but when it comes to creating their own independent learning environment and taking responsibility for their own learning, what is going to take priority is a big question.

To become successful adults, who are capable of adapting and re-inventing themselves, students need to realize that learning is their responsibility. How a student engages in learning depends on a type of intelligence as well as on socioeconomic, religious, and cultural factors. The engagement could come from a content that a student finds personally interesting, from an activity that stimulates a personal response, from the atmosphere that appeals to a student's emotion, or all of them at the same time. With all the variances, what stays constant is that it takes much more than one particular learning environment for a student to learn.

Locus of Control

When the idea of a school–family–community collaboration on a macro level is discussed with educators and parents, inevitably, the same objection surfaces: "I have no control over what happens outside of my immediate environment, so I am not wasting my efforts on trying."

This disposition is often based on prior experiences. Teachers frequently feel discouraged when their attempts to communicate with families on learning-related matters are met with an apparent disinterest. They feel that they have no way to control learning environments that a child enters when at home or other community locations. Parents are unsure of how much control they may have over their child's learning environment at school, often feeling excluded and unwelcome. Many complain that even their concerns related to a child's emotional security are frequently dismissed by teachers and school administrators, let alone any expertise-questioning feedback regarding learning.

A situation is considered controllable when one's voluntary responses have an impact on the situation (Seligman, 1992). However, people's own preconceptions often determine what they see as controllable. The concept of locus of control, in general terms, refers to one's belief about control over his or her environment. People who feel personally responsible for the things that happen to them are considered internals. Those who feel that everything is determined by forces beyond their control are considered externals. Although the locus of control is a relatively enduring disposition, it can be modified and influenced through experience (Findley & Cooper, 1983).

In the study that looked closely at the Abilene Paradox, a circumstance where a group of individuals agree to a course of action based on the theory that it is the best for the group, research showed that "individuals with high external locus are less likely to be committed to their organizations [. . .] they may feel unable to influence organizational decision making" [. . .] (Jatkevicius, 2010, p. 78).

This finding has a direct relevance to various stakeholders' commitment to co-create a learning environment. A long-time separation of schools and not-schools in the education of U.S. youth has created a "they vs. us" attitude, when both sides tend to exhibit a high external locus based on the belief that a child's learning environment at school/outside of school is guided by circumstances out of their control. This can weaken the commitment. In some cases, both families and educators can assume a high internal locus and not accept outside influence for the outcomes, no matter what that is.

Although to a certain degree, it is healthy to realize some limitations, as well as to take responsibility for one's own actions, neither assuming a "there is nothing I can do" attitude nor insisting on the entire control can create a powerful learning environment. In addition, intentions and design count for only so much in a learning environment, which is, as Tom Warger and Gregory Dobbin (2009) note, "a mix of the deliberate and the accidental, the conjunction of planned and unanticipated events" (p. 3). Thus, a macro learning environment should be seen as a sphere of influence where all stakeholders can influence decision making and outcomes without having absolute control.

A macro learning environment is built by all stakeholders—educators, students, parents, coaches, and leaders of various units and organizations—who comprise the entire community. Everyone has a certain level of control and responsibility for a learning environment that promotes the twenty-first-century skills and global understanding and helps children find their purpose and passion in this world.

To create such an environment, educational systems are called to nurture a very distinct culture within both micro and macro learning environments: a culture of partnerships. Chapter 3 will explore a shared vision, trust, decision making, stages of formation, and cultural forces as applied to the concept of a culture of partnerships.

TRY THIS

To get a general idea of where you stand on the locus of control personality dimension, consider taking this locus of control survey. A locus of control personality test was first created by Julian Rotter to assess individual internal or external reinforcement beliefs. Based on Rotter's idea, Terry Pettijohn, a professor in the psychology department in Mercyhurst College, Pennsylvania, has developed the tool described next (*Locus of Control*, n.d.).

Locus of Control Tool

Answer each question as T (true) or F (false):

1. I usually get what I want in life.
2. I need to be kept informed about news events.
3. I never know where I stand with other people.
4. I do not really believe in luck or chance.
5. I think that I could easily win a lottery.
6. If I do not succeed on a task, I tend to give up.
7. I usually convince others to do things my way.
8. People make a difference in controlling crime.
9. The success I have is largely a matter of chance.
10. Marriage is largely a gamble for most people.
11. People must be the master of their own fate.
12. It is not important for me to vote.
13. My life seems like a series of random events.
14. I never try anything that I am not sure of.
15. I earn the respect and honors I receive.
16. A person can get rich by taking risks.
17. Leaders are successful when they work hard.
18. Persistence and hard work usually lead to success.
19. It is difficult to know who my real friends are.
20. Other people usually control my life.

Scoring

5 points for each *False* answer on questions: 2, 3, 5, 6, 9, 10, 12, 13, 14, 16, 19, 20

5 points for each *True* answer on questions: 1, 4, 7, 8, 11, 15, 17, 18

Results

0–15 Very strong external locus of control
20–35 External locus of control
40–60 Both external and internal locus of control
65–80 Internal locus of control
85–100 Very strong internal locus of control

Chapter 2 Snapshot: CANVAS FOR LEARNING

FOCUS AREA	COMMON BELIEF	WHAT TO CONSIDER
Learning	Nature: Biology determines the intellectual characteristics with which children are born. Children have to be placed in instructional settings early.	Nature: The human brain is pliable: It is being shaped and re-shaped through interaction with the environment. Multiple intelligences—the extent to which learners learn, remember, and understand in different ways The superior learning in playful settings
	Nurture: Can affect learning but plays a secondary role in biology	Nurture: Learning is deeply connected to other processes and experiences affecting a child as a whole.
Learning Environment	A space, often within the walls of an educational institution, where students are expected to learn	A micro learning environment—a physically contained space controlled by the internal forces of this environment's providers A macro learning environment—the context of influences that come from all of the learning environments that a child enters

(continued)

Chapter 2 Snapshot (*continued*)

FOCUS AREA	COMMON BELIEF	WHAT TO CONSIDER
Responsibility	Teachers and administrators	Teachers, administrators, families, and community
Control	Teachers control a learning environment at schools. Parents control a learning environment at home. Teachers don't have any control over a home learning environment. Families don't have any control over a school learning environment.	No one has absolute control over any learning environment. A learning environment is a combination of influences; all stakeholders can influence decision making without having absolute control.

Chapter Three

A Culture of Partnerships

There is no "they." We are the "they." One team. United. All in the mission together. No barriers. No boundaries. Just open doors, open minds and an open culture rooted in trust.

—ISMs in Action

In the past few decades, the world has changed. Google provides abundant information in a matter of seconds, whereas old encyclopedias and dictionaries are collecting dust on shelves. Local neighborhoods are growing more diversified as people from different countries live next to each other. At work, adapting to frequent job changes and working with teams in various global locations are new norms.

Change is now one of the most popular words in the English language. It has been the subject of thousands of books, lectures, articles, and reforms, urging institutions and organizations to adjust their cultures and practices in response to challenges of our times. To confront the challenges of the future, however, it is broadly consented that the most powerful means that society has is education.

TO CHANGE OR NOT TO CHANGE?

It is a rather common thought among many educational leaders that schools don't transform society, but merely reflect it. Alan Singer, a professor of teacher education at Hofstra University in New York, offers a similar view:

There is a lot of talk about how schools can transform society. The Bush administration's education policy declared "No Child Left Behind," but of course many children are still left behind. Barack Obama demanded that schools lead his "Race to the Top," but it is not clear what direction he wants the schools and students to run. The reality is that schools reflect and reinforce society; they do not transform it. (as cited in Ravitch, 2014, November 8)

On the contrary, tectonic shifts did happen in our society, but thus far, education has failed to reflect them. It is quite possible that the Third and Fourth Industrial Revolutions have been happening within such a short timeframe and so rapidly that society as a whole has progressed unevenly, leaving many communities with the same mindset as has been there for many years. At the same time, children grow into the intellectual life around them (Vygotsky, 1978), and to ensure that all students develop twenty-first-century skills and dispositions, schools have to shape this intellectual life in local communities and their own organizations.

For quite a while, the U.S. K–12 education system has been under heavy criticisms coming from multiple sectors, including governmental, philanthropic, the marketplace, and the media, all calling for a transformational change. Just a quick search on *Amazon* identified 15,041 books on educational change, 12,136 on organizational change, and 564 on a change in educational culture. However, no substantial broad-scale change has occurred. Why could this be the case?

Organizational change is inseparable from personal change. Both organizations and individuals function according to their mental models—"deeply ingrained assumptions, generalizations, or even pictures and images that influence how we understand the world and how we take action" (Senge, 2006, p. 8). These mental models are an underlying root cause for unconscious "hidden commitments," as Kegan and Lahey (2009) define Immunity to Change, which compete and conflict with people's stated commitment to change.

Yong Zhao (2012) calls it a hangover of cultural evolution. The reason, he explains, we have a hard time letting go of the old system despite the obvious, is that it has "features that hold tremendous appeal to the human nature: our naturally evolved desire for orderliness, control, competitive advantage, and short-term immediate results" (p. 160). Another factor is our inability to "perceive large and distant changes" (p. 162).

Personal change is difficult. Organizational change is difficult. Educational change, requiring mental model shifts in various individuals (educators, parents, students, and community members) and in organizations in charge of education, is probably even more difficult. Education cannot be controlled entirely by one organization. It brings together stakeholders, whose commitment to change cannot be mandated by school administrators; it can only be nurtured.

Thus, although changes do happen inside discrete classrooms and schools, the only way for them to become transformative for the entire community is through a shared culture—a culture where all individual stakeholders are open to learn from each other as partners.

> This means involving everyone in the system in expressing their aspirations, building their awareness, and developing their capabilities together. In a school that learns, people who traditionally may have been suspicious of one another—parents and teachers, educators and local businesspeople, administrators and union members, people inside and outside the school walls, students and adults—recognize their common stake in each other's future and the future of their community. (Senge et al, 2012, p. 5)

A school learning orientation differs from a professional learning orientation. As Joyce Epstein and Karen Salinas (2004) note, a professional learning community relies on the teamwork of principals, teachers, and staff and can "greatly improve teaching, instruction, and professional relationships in a school, but it falls short of producing a true community of learners. In contrast, a school learning community includes educators, students, parents, and community partners who work together to improve the school and enhance students' learning opportunities" (p. 12).

To shape the intellectual life of a learning community, educational establishments need to become a source of awareness, influence, and change within their community, constructing and nurturing its macro learning environment. To do so, they must design intentional partnerships, wherein families, community members, and schools learn together, combine resources, and share decision-making power. This requires a substantial shift in how schools think of and interact with parents.

ADVERSARIES AND ADVOCATES

In March of 1928, *Child Study* magazine published an article written by Carleton Washburne, superintendent of schools in Winnetka, Illinois, largely known for his progressive educational innovation, Winnetka Plan. In his piece titled "The Public School and the Parent," Washburne shared something that pointed at the very core of a school–family tug-of-war for control in education.

> Principals and teachers could be aloof, holding parents at arm's length. Parents, on the other hand, could be opinionated, insisting that educators implement their recommendations. Those who joined home and school associations could be dismissed as politicians or social climbers. [...] Educators had to shed such

biased expectations [. . .] Schools needed both the confidence and the criticism of parents, and neither could be had unless the professionals respected the parents' right to make requests and express opinions. (as cited in Cutler III, 2000, p. 52)

Unfortunately, many educators, who at the time were some of the most educated workforce in the United States, didn't think that opinions of typically less educated parents, especially in non-English-speaking immigrant communities, could provide much contribution. For parents insisting on having some control over their children's schooling, options were limited to looking for the right school for their child. The president of the Progressive Education Association Stanwood Cobb, for example, urged parents to take more responsibility for identifying the quality of their children's schools:

The modern mother is distinctly interested in the education of her child, and is not willing to delegate this important matter to others. She must acquaint herself with the newest methods in education; she must study her child's school, analyzing it for its strengths and weaknesses. She must become qualified to choose the right school for her child. (as cited in Cutler III, 2000, p. 57)

This, of course, was almost a hundred years ago. Parents are much better educated now, in many cases, with college degrees comparable or superior to those of teachers'. Still, the mindset of superiority in knowing what is best for each child's learning and development is prevalent among educators.

On February 5, 2016, just a week after losing her son to flu, Melody Arabo, the 2014–15 Michigan Teacher of the Year, wrote an open letter on her blog to share a troubling story of her six-year-old twins' treatment by the school district where she taught. The boys were transferred from their home school to a segregated classroom for cognitively impaired on the other side of this large district, "regardless of the fact that they were successfully meeting their IEP [individualized education plan] goals in their general education classrooms, which we have mounds of evidence and data to prove," writes Arabo.

The boys' biggest challenge was their speech delay, speech apraxia, which prevented them from communicating the way other six-year-olds did. Since the district used assessments requiring students to use typical language, Arabo believes, the results inaccurately labeled her children as cognitively impaired. Of course, mistakes happen. The Arabo family asked district administrators to talk to the boys' teachers and support staff about their ability to grow as learners in the general education setting, but, surprisingly, this request was denied.

We've followed the chain of command that was recommended and have exhausted every avenue that we could think of in order to resolve these issues in a private and amicable manner. Our concerns have been chalked up to a difference in philosophical beliefs and making a fuss because we weren't getting what we want. But this is about so much more than just getting our way. It is about poor treatment of families who are already struggling with their children's challenges. . . .

I share this story because I know that there are so many others, across the state and nation, that have felt voiceless and powerless. . . . I share this because if this process has been so challenging for me, a valued employee of the district, a State Teacher of the Year, and a member of Governor's Task Force on Special Education, I can only imagine how hard it must be for families without titles or resources or connections. It is time for change. (Arabo, 2016, February 5)

Feeling voiceless and powerless is likely to resonate with many parents who tried to advocate for their children in schools, and not just in Special Education. The biggest problem with creating family–school partnerships, as Harvard professor Karen Mapp points out, is that school staff often "look down on the families they serve, seeing them as hindrances rather than as potential partners" (as cited in Taylor, 2015, September 8). Mapp's perception of the problem between parents and schools resembles the one expressed by progressive educators in the 1920s.

To this day, many school leaders are unable to form partnerships with families, because they don't believe that parents know what is best for their children and, instead, create systems that protect schools from parental opinions and requests. In return, parents feel neither respected by schools nor inclined to trust the expertise of educators. Their option once again is to choose the right school or the right teacher for their child. The main difference between the 1920s and the approaching 2020s, however, is that then, most schools could function rather well without any input from parents; thus, alienation of families was self-sustaining. In the upcoming era of the Fourth Industrial Revolution, this can no longer be the case.

Re-designing schools' culture toward a culture of partnerships is not an easy process. There are many hidden commitments inherited from the past. Although there might be a desire *for* change, no one really desires *to* change. However, without changing minds, change is not possible. Howard Gardner (2006) sees changing minds as situations where "individuals or groups abandon the way in which they have customarily thought about an issue of importance and henceforth conceive of it in a new way" (p. 2).

Actions are reflections of thoughts. What school and district leaders, and consequently, teachers, believe about parents, their attitudes, aptitudes, and most importantly, their roles in learning, will translate into their actions and reactions toward parents. As school leaders and educators are called to be agents of change "who bring about a mental shift" (Gardner, 2006, p. 2) in others, the transformation needs to start with their own minds and mental models.

THE MINDSET OF PARTNERSHIPS

There are likely very few, if any, educators who are not aware of the positive effects that partnering with families and community organizations could have on student learning. Most school and district leaders do understand this fact: Parents are important in improving and maintaining student learning. Family engagement interconnects multiple settings where children learn—home, school, after-school programs, and the community—making families essential in creating a positive macro learning environment.

Forming partnerships, however, is not the same as working with families. It involves creating new relationships among people, which means realizing the give-and-take nature of any relationship:

• What do we wish to gain by embracing partnerships?
• What are we willing to give?

A culture of partnerships entails that all parties share the ownership of what is being accomplished. It is not about parents or community organizations "helping" schools in educating their children. It is about all stakeholders feeling responsible and accountable for creating the best learning environment for all students.

The mindset of partnerships starts with a deeply seeded belief that schools, and therefore educators, serve the public, and parents are an essential part of that public, with a huge vested interest—their children. This mindset recognizes the fact that all families have some skills to help their children succeed through K–12 and beyond, and most parents are experts when it comes to their children. This dictates respect for parental insights regarding their children's physical, instructional, social, and emotional needs.

For educators, and especially school and district leaders, there might be a need for a shift in the locus of control from the high internal toward the middle, allowing for sharing power and resources. "In the best of all possible worlds," write Adams and Christenson (2000), "the family-school relationship would be based not only on two-way communication, cooperation, and coordination, but also on collaboration" (p. 478). Collaboration is never a one-way flow.

A partnership, by its very nature, also implies interdependence, which, in a school setting, may mean letting go of control and becoming dependent on a parent. "Regardless of how much formal power any given role has in a school community, all participants must remain dependent on others to achieve desired outcomes and feel empowered by their efforts" (Bryk & Schneider,

2003, p. 42). This requires trust in parents and community members as partners. Thus, the cornerstone of this mindset is the presence of trust among people who are working together in a peer setting.

Trust, especially in a partnership, is a multi-faceted concept that includes benevolence, honesty, openness, reliability, and competence (Tschannen-Moran, 2014). Involving parents in district or school governance, for example, mandates trust in their benevolence—that they will be driven by the common goal. Genuinely listening to parental perspectives, and most notably, taking these perspectives into consideration in future actions on academic matters, takes openness and trust in their competence. Reliability comes through keeping promises, no matter how insignificant they might seem. In trust-based partnerships, following through is viewed as a symbol of honor and promises are kept at all costs.

Multiple research findings, including a longitudinal study of 400 elementary schools, have shown that relational trust plays the major part in building productive educational communities (Henderson & Mapp, 2002). In a culture of partnerships, quantity and quality of trust serve as a binding substance that allows all partners to work in tandem. All parties—schools, families, and community members—share the responsibility for building trust. But those who hold the official power within schools and classrooms have to set the tone and lead by example.

A CULTURE OF PARTNERSHIPS DESIGN

A traditional definition of a *culture* is a "set of shared attitudes, values, goals, and practices that characterizes an institution, organization, or group. Considered by social scientists to be the 'collective programming of the mind'" (Morris et al, n.d., p. 3), culture is shared: It is formed on the foundation of a shared set of beliefs that determine expected behavior. Each individual member of the organization "may have his or her own particular beliefs about a specific element, but ultimately there is an overarching belief that becomes part of the culture" (Morris et al, n.d., p. 3).

A culture of partnerships can be defined as a shared mindset within educational establishments that results in attitudes, values, goals, and practices that are directed at building a powerful macro learning environment, wherein families, community organizations, and other educational establishments are committed to sharing the responsibility for children's learning. It is important to consider the elements of a culture of partnerships as a shared framework that takes into consideration the multiple contexts in which children learn, from birth through adulthood.

A culture of partnerships is based on three core principles:

- It is aimed at promoting children's learning anywhere, any time.
- Education of children is seen as a shared responsibility: Schools, other community agencies and organizations, and families are committed to collaborating in meaningful ways to provide a coherent powerful learning environment for children.
- Collaboration entails steadfast commitment to children above stakeholders' roles or personal/organizational interests.

Common Vision

Any partnership should begin with a common vision—a realistic and appealing picture of the future where all stakeholders want to be. Admittedly, administrators want to see a supportive teaching and learning environment for their teachers and students, whereas parents and community organizations might have a desire for schools with a more rounded understanding of their children's capabilities and more opportunities for their academic and personal growth. Ideally, though, the vision of schools, community agencies and organizations, and families working together to better student learning should appeal to all.

A classroom's, a school's, or a district's vision might be context specific and geared toward a particular set of children and needs, but "to be effective, the form of involvement should be focused on improving achievement and be designed to engage families and students in developing specific knowledge and skill," advise Anne Henderson and Karen Mapp (2002, p. 38) in their report *A New Wave of Evidence*. A vision that is learning driven and can be easily understood by all partners is what is needed.

Sharing Responsibilities and Power

Schools, community agencies and organizations, and families in a partnership have to mutually agree on their roles and obligations and clarify their expectations about the obligations of others. Parents' obligations first and foremost are to their children's learning and well-being, and then, to specific goals that their organization or program attempts to achieve within schools. Teachers' obligations are to a group of children and their parents in a particular classroom. School and district administrators' obligations are much wider; they encompass all of the school community and entail creating an effective, safe learning and teaching environment in their schools. This, of course, includes ensuring learning opportunities for an individual child and facilitating the work of parents.

For teachers, respectful sharing of responsibilities often means providing some guidance and information on the learning process and classroom expectations, but letting parents choose how they incorporate this at home. It also means trusting parents to do what is right for their child and not casting judgments or dismissing their concerns regarding learning as ignorant. For superintendents and principals, respectful sharing of responsibilities lies in defining and maintaining a line that separates their areas of control from areas where control shifts back to parents. Leaders with a partnership mindset provide their partners with some guidelines based on district policies, for example, but trust parents or organizations to control how to run a program or deal with their own matters.

In other words, administrators should be aware of work done by their partners, but they should rely on them to make competent decisions and trust their integrity in this process. In addition, partners might need to have access to direct communication with school or district staff either at staff meetings or electronically. Many administrators don't allow such access. Principals and superintendents who are partners, however, embrace parent and community leaders as part of their teams, open a communication flow, and allow direct connections to take place.

A good example for understanding a complex juncture of roles and responsibilities among multiple stakeholders in a partnership is collaboration between school districts, families, and local health and social service agencies to meet needs of all students and ensure that they can learn. In such a partnership, as suggested by ASCD (2007), schools can be responsible for making sure that every child has an adult mentor and for re-designing school schedules to allow adequate time for mentoring and professional development that supports effective mentoring programs.

Schools can also provide healthy food options, physical education programs, recess for elementary students, health education programs, and an environment that enables students and staff to practice healthy behaviors. Districts' educational programs should include social and emotional learning and promote school-based activities, such as peer mediation and conflict resolution, for a positive school climate.

Communities, on the other hand, are called to collaborate with school districts and health/social service agencies to ensure access to health services and learning opportunities in both school and community settings. Parents could help develop extracurricular and after-school activities that incorporate community experiences, provide opportunities for community-based learning through apprenticeships with local businesses, become qualified mentors to students, and support flexible pathways to graduation by providing community-based opportunities to demonstrate achievement (ASCD, 2007, pp. 21–25).

Removing Barriers

In his book, *Creative Schools* (2015), Ken Robinson describes the experience of his co-author and highly regarded writer and editor, Lou Aronica, with his children's schools, when he offered his help with school writing projects. Year after year, Aronica's offers were declined. What frustrates many parents is how hesitant school systems could be when it comes to accepting the expertise of parents to offer enhancements to their programs. "Most districts don't make a great use of—or even shun—these resources" (p. 211).

The main objection to letting parents contribute to student learning at schools that comes from educators often boils down to their "hidden commitment" to old insecurity: Parents don't trust them to be trained, capable experts, knowing what's best for their children. Thus, parents who wish to be involved have to have ulterior reasons, such as to see how their child is doing compared with others; to share with their neighbors that so and so's child is a terrible reader; or to gossip about a teacher at the bus stop, telling other parents to request for someone else next year. Ironically, erecting barriers doesn't solve this problem; it makes it worse. Most parents talk to each other, because they are frequently hesitant to say anything to teachers, expecting a defensive reaction and potential repercussions for their child.

There is a difference between being an expert and being always right. Expertise of any kind doesn't appear on its own. It is a result of trials, errors, and learning from mistakes. Parents may be right or wrong, but so may teachers. If both of them do their best for the same child, however, neither educators nor parents should be afraid to give and receive feedback on what works or doesn't work in the learning process. In fact, many studies showed that when schools listen to parents' ideas and act on them, they create better learning environments (Robinson, 2015).

Parents are likely the most untapped resource in education to which schools are forced to turn when something goes wrong. Families, however, do want to contribute when everything is right as well. Most parents desire what is best for their children, including their learning, so they want to be part of the school community. Teachers' expertise is not challenged by parents' offers to contribute to classroom learning. Likewise, parents' expertise regarding their child is not challenged by teachers' suggestions for his or her learning at home. Only together, combining their unique vantage points, schools and families can establish true expertise in educating each child.

When the Road Map Project, the project based on the belief that collective effort is necessary to make large-scale change in schools, came to Kent, Washington, to form a design, the team of teachers and parents gathered substantial evidence that community organizations and parents themselves are "the experts on their own interests, needs and priorities—and that schools can be leaders in achieving more effective partnerships by recognizing parents' strengths, accounting for cultural context, and changing policies or practices to remove barriers" (Chen, Ishimaru, & Lott, 2015, July 28, para. 6). There are some steps that can facilitate removal of barriers:

- Developing a family–community engagement strategy with representation from a variety of stakeholder groups
- Creating new district or school policies that would allow parents and community organizations to take part in education and instruction, based on their credentials and expertise
- Building district capacity for partnerships through creating partnership-centered programs, positions, and professional development for administrators and staff
- Ensuring reporting, learning, and accountability for family and community engagement
- Restructuring decision-making processes, committees, and groups to include representation from major stakeholders, especially families

CULTURAL FORCES AS DIRECTED TOWARD PARTNERSHIPS

In his book, *Intellectual Character* (2002), Ron Ritchhart delineated the eight cultural forces that act as shapers of any group's cultural dynamics: time, opportunities, routines and structures, language, modeling, interactions and relationships, physical environment, and expectations. Later, in *Creating Cultures of Thinking* (2015), Ritchhart outlined how leveraging these cultural forces can enable an educational establishment to create a positive collegial culture. Although his original application of these forces was directed toward creating cultures of thinking, the same principles can be applied to any organizational culture, regardless of location or purpose. If educators take them into consideration, cultural forces will guide them toward achieving a culture of partnerships in their schools, classrooms, and communities.

Time

There are very few school administrators who could say that they regularly build in time for reaching out to families or community organizations and agencies with a purpose of sharing current practices, explaining shifts in instruction and learning, creating a new program, or partnering on a specific project. Even elementary teachers spend a minimum amount of time communicating with families, and this amount often drops to none at secondary schools.

Time nowadays is a precious commodity; how we spend it communicates our priorities and beliefs. Regularly, time should be allocated for proactive family and community engagement by regularly scheduling slots for information sharing, two-way communication, collaborative discussions, and follow-up.

Opportunities

Most parents want to support children's learning at home, but they often don't know how to do it. As many changes have been occurring in how schools approach curriculum, methodology, and student assessment, there is a gap between parents' own educational experiences, stemming from decades ago, and their children's learning. Parents need to understand the learning process and their role as partners in their children's education.

Schools have to provide purposeful activities that require families and community organizations and agencies to engage in student learning. Training or mentoring sessions for parents could offer good learning opportunities. In addition, affording parents and community members opportunities to take initiative on learning-related matters is vital in forging productive partnerships.

Routines and Structures

Any unit within an educational organization—from a classroom to a district—has to have developed, clear guiding routines on how to build partnerships with different stakeholders. If a parent or an organization shows an initiative to partner in any way, no matter to whom this initiative is originally communicated, the response has to be consistent. Every team member, from a teacher aide to a superintendent, has to know what steps to follow. Ideally, there should be developed district, school, or classroom processes (routines) for family and/or community engagements, as well as structures that support them.

Language

There is nothing that tells a story of a culture faster than the language used within an organization. Partnerships are about collaboration, joint ownership, and collegial relationships. It's not "us" versus "them" or "we" versus "you." It is about us. *We* are decision makers. Use of conditional language versus the absolute language, such as "it might be" versus "it is," communicates openness to various perspectives and evolving thinking, which are always present in powerful learning environments.

Modeling

"Leaders lead by example" could be a good definition of modeling. Modeling comes through one's actions and behaviors that embed the essence of a particular culture. To be partners and communicate expectations of partnership behaviors to families and community, educators and administrators should act like partners. This implies transparency in sharing information, listening for understanding, being accountable for their part, following through, and enabling joined decision making. For the process of collaboration to take place, modeling of who they are as partners is essential for leaders.

Interactions and Relationships

Relationships have always been the main driving force behind human actions and interactions. When people are nice to each other and non-confrontational, their relationships are congenial. Many teachers and school administrators strive toward building congenial relationships both inside and outside of school walls.

Although, of course, there is nothing wrong with being nice, a culture of partnerships cannot be sustained by congeniality alone. It requires collegial relationships, based on mutual ownership and shared responsibility for decision making. People have to see each other as partners, rather than as friends or acquaintances, and value each other's contributions of ideas and resources within distinctly collegial relationships.

Physical (and Virtual) Environments

Physical and virtual environments can shape cultural beliefs and understandings by influencing perceptions, interactions, communications, and, as a result, behaviors of people. To expand a culture of partnerships, partnerships have to be made visible and known. Schools and school districts can display their partnerships with families and organizations by inviting and honoring parent leaders and other partners during important district events, such as a senior graduation.

Places of faith, community agents, and parental organizations should invite principals, superintendents, and educators to their important events. Schools and organizations can utilize their social media to share each other's posts and information. Partnerships can be made visible to the community by consistently displaying affiliations.

Expectations

Various stakeholders may have different expectations about partnerships, their dynamics and outcomes. Organizations and schools often have contrasting agenda based on their own goals and priorities. Thus, it has to be established from the very start that setting an agenda of shared decision making with a focus on improving student learning is the top priority for all partners.

STAGES OF A CULTURE OF PARTNERSHIP FORMATION

There are three factors that drive families and local communities toward education-centered partnerships:

- Efficacy—knowledge and confidence to contribute
- Opportunities—openings to apply knowledge or skills
- Influence—making a difference by affecting decision making in a particular classroom, school, or district

Each of these factors can be engaged and continuously enriched at various levels of educational leadership during each stage of a culture of partnerships formation. Depending on the main goal of what is being accomplished, there are three distinct stages to this process, namely, Creating Awareness, Seeking Engagement, and Supporting Collaboration.

Creating Awareness, first, or passive, stage in the formation of a culture of partnerships within a school or a district, to some degree, could be regarded as a preparatory stage. Its main goal is to create awareness through providing information and sharing ideas. Creating Awareness is the stage for schools to nurture important understandings about changes in education, instruction, and curriculum and why they occur. As parents and community members become familiar with the direction the schools are taking, they are more likely to actively participate in learning-related tasks.

Seeking Engagement, or experiencing, stage brings around an action. It is important to note that the term *engagement* in this case refers to a wide scope of activities conducted at school, home, or community locations that include anything that contributes to improving a macro learning environment. By making parents and other family members feel welcome at school, providing multiple opportunities for families to get involved in learning, and enabling participation, teachers and school leaders can achieve an ongoing engagement.

Human beings, no matter whether they are parents, educators, or students, learn best when they can try things for themselves. Whether it is common core standards and associated teaching and learning practices, cultures of thinking, project-based learning, or any other innovative framework or methodology practiced in schools, there is no better way to engage parents in their student's learning than letting them experience it for themselves.

Supporting Collaboration is a partnership stage. When families, community organizations and agencies, and other stakeholders are aware of the learning that takes place in schools, the rationale behind this learning, and how it looks like in implementation, they gain valuable insight. This insight allows them to realize schools' needs to successfully continue in this direction. At this stage, parents, parental and community organizations, and local businesses are ready to enter collaboration, either by invitation or on their own initiative. The relationships among all of the stakeholders enter the collegial state, whereas sharing power, resources, and common goals are supported by schools' infrastructure.

When working toward a culture of partnerships, it is good to remember that stages of its formation are not self-contained. Rather, a stage is a milestone in a continuous progress. In most cases, educators simultaneously create awareness, engage parents and community, and create opportunities to collaborate. To understand what makes collaboration different from engagement and engagement different from awareness, the following ways to respond to the need to adopt a new socio-emotional learning platform in a school or district can provide some guidance:

1. The principal (superintendent) selects the platform and informs his or her teachers and staff. Parents most likely never officially hear anything.
2. The principal (superintendent) and staff discuss options and collaboratively select the platform. Parents are informed and offered some general information.
3. The principal (superintendent) and staff discuss options and collaboratively select the platform. Parents are informed, and learning opportunities (training, workshops) are offered to all parents throughout a year.
4. The principal (superintendent), staff, parent leaders (or delegates selected by parents), and a local counselor discuss options and collaboratively select the platform. The principal (superintendent) and parent leaders develop a plan for creating awareness and providing learning opportunities to parents. They are responsible for carrying out different aspects of this plan.

In these scenarios, there are obvious differences in how administrators think about families/community and their roles. The first option allows for no internal or external input. Most likely, collaboration doesn't exist and there is a gap even between administrators and staff. The role of families in these circumstances is often marginalized. The second scenario is most likely to happen at the Creating Awareness stage. There is an internal collegial culture, which is accompanied by understanding that it is important to keep parents informed so that they might support these efforts at home.

The third scenario happens when schools begin to see parents as their necessary collaborators at home and become intentional about sharing knowledge and developing know-how. This is the Seeking Engagement stage. Finally, the last scenario is that of the collaboration stage, when schools see parents as equal partners in matters related to their children's education; they share decision-making power and responsibility for making this work.

REFLECT ON THIS

For District and School Leaders

1. How do I think of parents' role in the operation of the school/district?
2. How often do I speak to my staff about family and community partnerships? Do we dedicate time to brainstorm ideas about working with families and the community?
3. What change can I incorporate in my language to reflect the idea of partnerships?
4. Are partnerships with families and the community visible in my school/district?
5. A partnership is based on the give-and-take philosophy. As an administrator, what am I prepared to give in a partnership?
6. If partners are equally responsible for making decisions, how do I share power in decision making beyond just soliciting and considering parental perspectives and help?
7. At what stage of a culture of partnerships continuum is my school or district now? What prevents me from moving to the next stage?
8. What is one change that I can implement tomorrow to take another step toward a culture of partnerships?

For Educators

1. How do I see the role of parents in my classroom? Do I ask for their help or seek their expertise?
2. Do I build my communication and interactions with parents and community members to create personal liking or to promote a shared responsibility for education of our students? How does my language reflect this?
3. Do I catch myself saying "Yes, but . . . " when I am faced with some potential criticism from families? What can I do better to keep an open mind?
4. How much time do I dedicate to building a learning community with my class parents?

5. What opportunities for learning do I offer parents?
6. What expectations do I communicate to families regarding their roles as partners in their children's learning? Have we established an understanding of what this role is?
7. What is one change that I can implement tomorrow to take another step toward a culture of partnerships?

Chapter 3 Snapshot: A CULTURE OF PARTNERSHIPS CONTINUUM

CREATING AWARENESS	SEEKING ENGAGEMENT	SUPPORTING COLLABORATION
Goal: Building knowledge and understanding	Building consensus	Building shared decision making and ownership
Rationale: Removing separation	Promoting participation	Promoting collegiality
Focus: Supplying information	Supplying education	Requesting and utilizing expertise Sharing resources and power
Action: Creating communication systems	Creating learning opportunities	Creating capacity for collaboration and partnership opportunities
Schools' position: Schools are speaking Seeking acceptance	Schools are teaching and coaching Seeking feedback	Schools are listening Seeking direction
Mindset: Maintaining *independence* from families and the community	Acknowledging *dependence* on families and the community	Realizing *interdependence* between schools, families, and the community
Factors that drive engagement: Efficacy—knowledge and confidence to contribute	Efficacy—knowledge and confidence to contribute Opportunities—openings to apply knowledge or skills	Opportunities—openings to apply knowledge or skills Influence—making a difference by affecting decision making in a particular classroom, school, or district

Chapter Four

Creating Awareness

In vain have you acquired knowledge if you have not imparted it to others.

—Deuteronomy Rabbah

The initial step to constructing a powerful learning environment is developing awareness within the educational community and the public that re-orienting education to meet the needs of the twenty-first century is essential. Families, community organizations and agencies have to become aware of the critical linkages between education and other factors that affect a child's ability to learn. This awareness often creates a start for shifting educational responsibility toward partnerships.

By not giving this step the importance it deserves, schools run a risk of creating an impression that they are not capable of fulfilling their purpose in educating children and youth, and, consequently, have little chance of forming effective partnerships. On the other hand, when all stakeholders realize the need for a shift from rote learning to critical thinking, skill building, and application of knowledge, they are likely to recognize how schools depend on communities and families for support at home or through local programs.

For a lot of classroom educators, creating awareness is not anything new. For quite a while, the focus of family–school communications has been on building teacher–parent connections. Many teachers are good communicators, which truly makes a difference in how parents feel about their children's learning. What is important to understand here is that teachers cannot and should not be the only spokespeople on behalf of schools. There is a need for a comprehensive communication system within a school district.

School administrators and district leaders must become agents of change by delivering a consistent flow of communication about the new instructional practices that schools are undertaking, how they benefit children, and what is required from families and communities to become schools' partners in education. A communication system can only be as good as educators and administrators' commitment to contribute to its success.

An effective awareness system consists of multiple components and is executed by various stakeholders within schools and districts. Planning and maintaining effectiveness of the system call for teamwork—from teachers to principals to superintendents and parent leaders. Everyone needs to collaborate and contribute toward preparing the fertile soil for partnerships to grow.

CREATING AWARENESS SYSTEMS

Teachers are often the first to connect with families on education-related matters. There are many ways in which educators can do this nowadays. Some favor more traditional methods, such as weekly printed or electronic newsletters sent home with students or via e-mail. Some teachers create their own websites and blogs that feature classroom pictures, schedules, events, and reminders. There are also many relatively new avenues, such as Facebook pages, Twitter, Instagram, as well as downloadable applications (apps) that are made specifically for communications with students and families.

An increasing number of K–12 teachers are turning to free online and mobile applications to communicate with digitally savvy parents. *Remind*, for example, is a digital communication tool that allows one to schedule messages; *Edublogs* is a blogging platform that is designed specifically for teachers; and *ClassDojo* provides many ways to reach out to students and their families. Social media and YouTube also come handy to create awareness at schools. According to the National School Public Relations Association (NSPRA, 2011, August 26) survey, already in 2011, parents' preferred delivery methods included direct communication in electronic/Internet-based formats.

One way or the other, communication, in some degree, is currently being practiced by most educators. The important differentiation here, however, is not how information is being delivered, but what types of information educators provide. For the most part, teachers communicate organizational content. From a journalistic standpoint, they focus on answering the questions "what," "when," "where," and "who": What happened or is going to happen? Who was/is involved? When and where it occurred or is going to occur?

On the other hand, content preferences by parents from teachers include updates on how well their children are doing and how they can help them do better (NSPRA, 2011, August 26, para. 5). To provide insights in these areas, educators have to consider *why* and *how*—why children are doing a specific activity, how something is being taught, and, more importantly, how it all relates to the learning process.

The Learning Process

Before anything else, parents desire to know how to help children when they experience difficulties. Parents often feel that to provide guidance to their children, they need to be "experts" in subjects requiring help. The learning process, however, is not about curriculum or information; it is about applying prior knowledge, making new connections, and persevering despite difficulties. A steady stream of communication from a teacher, focused on the process of learning, is essential.

The initial parent communication should clearly state expectations of learning, believes Howard Andress, a sixth-grade advanced math teacher from Sashabaw Middle School in Michigan. Before a school year even begins, Andress provides his class parents with a list of learning habits that he expects from his students:

- Be an active participant in class discussions.
- Listen to and absorb the thoughts of others.
- Develop perseverance.
- Have a growth mindset.
- Be curious and celebrate the struggle.
- Ask learning questions.

Andress places special importance on making parents aware of what specifically they can do to assist their child, what language they should use to initiate independent discovery, and how to be effective coaches. His *First Communiqué*, sent to all of his students' parents, sets expectations of productive struggle within the learning process and provides answers to many *why's* that parents are likely to have (see Textbox 4.1).

To be effective coaches at home, parents need to become experts in the learning process itself. "Parents' recollection of the rules for the Pythagorean Theorem, for example, may be somewhat vague, but they can trigger discovery in their child using a certain line of questioning and prompts to reveal to the child aspects of the topic that he or she already knows but is not accessing at the moment" (Bokas & Andress, 2016, March 24, para. 6). Ideally, teachers provide an overview of assignments and topics, including notes and comments that offer some indication of the associated learning behaviors, on a regular basis.

The *Why* and the *How*

Parents need to understand the *why* behind the *how*. For most adults, whose schooling took place in the 1980s or 1990s, an attempt to help their children with school work often leads to the realization that drastic changes have

---

Textbox 4.1

WELCOME BACK—FIRST COMMUNIQUÉ

Howard Andress, Sixth-Grade Advanced Math Teacher

Sashabaw Middle School, MI

New Challenges!

Your Advanced Math student will face countless challenges and opportunities this year: a new year, a new building, and a new structure to their school experience. With change and challenge, students may experience moments of frustration and anxiety. This is normal and an aspect of the adjustment. However, they will soon, if not immediately, find Advanced Math to be both challenging and exhilarating. It will be an enjoyable experience for all of us: I am eager to begin and am looking forward to a great year!

Tips: When your child says, "I don't get it!"

- The problem may be that your child misread the problem. Try this: "What do you think the question is asking?" You may want to read the item together.
- Your child may not understand what the question is asking, so say, "What do you think you are *supposed* to do?"
- Help your child to "think the problem through." Have him/her explain to you what happened in class by saying, "Explain the problems that you did in class today and use your notebook to help."
- "Two heads are better than one." Children, just like us, often work through their confusion and develop better understanding if they work with a friend. Suggest, "Why don't you call _____ and ask if he/she got the same answer you did? Ask your friend to explain how he/she solved the problem." Group work, one of our common approaches in class, involves sharing strategies and answers. Cheating is telling each other the answers without doing the work. One of our key words in class is *collaboration*.

Many times, children say they don't understand, when in reality they may understand most of the concept, yet have some confusion about a small portion of the idea/procedure. Children have difficulty being precise in figuring out what they don't understand. Say to them, "Do the homework the best you can. I know effort is important, and you need to show your teacher you are trying to figure this out. Even if you get it wrong, you can show your teacher how much you do understand. When you don't try and do not attempt, your teacher will not be able to help you." Above all—get something down on paper!

Follow up the next day by asking, "How did you do on that assignment? What did you learn? What strategies can you use next time? Do you need to see your teacher for extra help?"

You're a partner in the learning process. You may relearn some interesting math concepts in the process (nice bonus).

occurred in a philosophy of education within the previous twenty to thirty years, influencing what and how students are taught. Consequently, the majority of parents and community members may not have a good grasp on current educational practices and, most importantly, on the reasons why they have changed.

When parents encounter an emphasis on thinking and developing twenty-first century dispositions, application of skills, group discussions, no grades, alternative assessments, minimizing teaching and maximizing learning, and accordingly, less homework or classwork sheets showing up at home, it can be very confusing. Not surprisingly, "both parents and non-parents listed the rationale/reasons for decisions made by the school district and curriculum/ educational options . . . in the top tier of content requests" (NSPRA, 2011, August 26, para. 7).

Families nowadays face unprecedented amounts of education-related decisions, often navigating a complex labyrinth of new learning opportunities. Thus, a constant flow of quality information is a must to keep a community abreast on what is important in learning. Though greatly appreciated, teachers' efforts alone cannot suffice. School and district leaders need to develop communication strategies to nurture understanding of innovative educational practices among families and community members throughout a school year. Most school districts have official websites, Twitter and Facebook accounts, and YouTube channels. All of these can be productively used for creating awareness.

School and District Websites

Websites have been traditionally used by schools and school districts to support the culture and brand of their schools. The new website designs, adopted by many districts, permit parents, community members, and students to find school and teacher web pages, school and classroom calendars, academic resources, menus, and transportation routes quickly and easily. Many websites also provide an increasing number of school-related documents and reports as well as drafts of minutes and agenda packets for school board meetings.

As comprehensive as they may be, school websites are only rarely utilized to create community awareness about educational shifts, and, primarily, they are geared toward people with children in the schools. This leaves the larger community unaware. It shouldn't come as a surprise then when districts lose votes on bond and tax measures. "With the vast majority of districts that are successful in getting funding from their community, it's because those districts have done their homework far in advance to build a connection," expressed Ann Flynn, director of education technology and state association services for the National School Boards Association (NSBA) (as cited in Gordon, 2012, June 19).

To build a connection, in addition to district-related information, websites should offer education- and learning-related insights: for example, the "What's New in Education" section. If updated regularly, this section can showcase innovative learning as well as communicate district needs to ensure that students can enjoy such learning. Success stories from other districts that met student learning needs by partnering with families and communities can be posted and shared with all stakeholders.

More than being merely a space to post information, websites can become a barometer of a community's responsiveness to new ideas. Offering surveys and provocative topics in search of feedback is a good way to gauge this. A social media directory that lists all administrator, teacher, school, and classroom Twitter handles, as well as links to parent–teacher association/parent–teacher organization (PTA/PTO) Facebook pages and Twitter accounts, will enable stakeholders to join them on social media and expand awareness further.

Social Media

Sharing school news and showcasing programs are typically the main reasons for social media use by school districts. However, district and school Facebook pages or Twitter feeds make it very easy to provide information on new educational research and methodology as well as on the rationale behind them. Social media also give schools a platform for inviting a dialog with members of the community, clarifying information, and answering questions.

Assessing how successful school districts utilize social media to educate parents and the community, Dan Gordon (2012, June 19) gives an example of the Klein Intermediate School District (ISD) in Texas that stepped up its social media presence, posting stories of learning on Facebook and inviting public comments. In the first year, the posts drew more than 3,000 "likes." Along with Facebook updates, at least one tweet a day, ranging from news on a spelling bee or a history day event to links to educational articles, was posted on Twitter.

There are many reputable websites, blogs, and online publications that offer resources on various aspects of learning, the whole child, and instructional practices. Growing out of the understanding that to make informed decisions parents need help finding quality resources, *Getting Smart*, for example, partnered with the Nellie Mae Education Foundation and the Huffington Post to create a popular parent blog series, *Smart Parents*, where both parents and educators share their stories and ideas. This blog is targeted specifically to families and may be insightful to many teachers and parents alike.

Edutopia and ASCD's *InService* and *Edge* blogs are also good sources to obtain a wide range of helpful information and real stories of learning from all over the country and beyond. Reading such stories opens the community to a much wider understanding of educational complexity in the context of the global world.

Video Websites and Public Television

It always has a stronger impact when people see and hear something than just read about it. Districts can utilize their local public access channels to broadcast interviews or Q&A sessions with superintendents, other district administrators, faculty members, educational thought leaders, and members of the community on topics of interest or concern in these particular locations. Clarkston Community Schools in Michigan, for instance, collaborated with the district PTA Council and Independence Television to begin *The Future of Learning* (Bokas, 2014–2016) public television series in hopes to share the district's educational philosophy with the community.

Episodes recorded on the show targeted various aspects of education, from global competence and twenty-first-century skills to teaching for big under-standings and learning by doing. *The Future of Learning Field* episodes cap-tured practices inside classrooms and included conversations with students about their learning. District educators, administrators, students, and parents appeared on the show to share their views on learning.

Skype technology allowed the community to hear from the Harvard University researchers such as David Perkins, Ron Ritchhart, and Carrie James. As the show grew and expanded, it brought in perspectives from the ISD and state superintendents, state legislators, state PTA leaders, and a president of one of Michigan's universities. The episodes were broadcast on the local channel, whereas links to their YouTube versions were widely shared through various social media. The impact on the community was palatable.

Short video clips and recordings of classroom practices and student work are always good ways to create awareness. Teacher- and student-created vid-eos can be incorporated into instructional practices, shared with parents, and used for professional development. In addition to YouTube, there are other video websites that could be used for these purposes: Vimeo, Yahoo Screen, Hulu, Vine, and a number of others.

GETTING THROUGH

The most common complaint that educators have when it comes to offering awareness building information to families is that parents, or community members for this matter, often ignore information supplied by educators. There is a lot of truth to this. In the world, where our attention is constantly being pulled in multiple directions, a competition for people's time is fierce. In order to dedicate any portion of it to reading for understanding, rather than quickly skipping over information, parents have to find it personally relevant and important to them.

The good news is that schools have a great "competitive advantage"— children. Every parent, as can be assumed, cares about his or her children. Teachers or school administrators can capitalize on this relevance to create awareness of new educational ideas and the direction that schools are taking. Although there is no guarantee that all parents and community members can be reached at all times, there are a number of factors that might help with establishing relevance and overcoming the "getting through" barrier.

A "Story" Factor

To be effective, not only does communication have to be interesting to read and easy to understand but it should also connect to an important "BIG understanding," as David Perkins (2014) defines universal values and questions that most human beings contemplate in their lives. In other words, it has to grab the reader and make him or her think about what is important in life. Thus, one of the techniques that can be especially useful in education is telling stories and connecting them to big learning *why's*.

Stories are tools of power; they can persuade and move people to action. Jennifer Aaker (Harnessing the Power of Stories, n.d.), a professor of marketing at Stanford Graduate School of Business, shares that stories are approximately 22 times more memorable than facts or figures alone. They are effective tools to advocate for ideas, especially when facts and figures are also weaved into this story. Anyone, from a teacher to a district leader, can tell stories about children and their learning in connection to a larger purpose.

Michelle Simecek (*Sharing a Story*), a Michigan elementary teacher, took the time to narrate a classroom experience with the purpose of sharing with parents an important example of meaningful learning. Her story highlighted students as human beings who made a difference in the lives of others. It gave parents immediate insight into the culture of the school and the classroom; it also established a connection and a common purpose for the work that schools and families can do together. Such messages don't come often from teachers, but they elevate education tremendously (see Textbox 4.2).

Textbox 4.2

SHARING A STORY—EMAIL TO CLASS PARENTS

Michelle Simecek, Third-Grade Teacher,

Bailey Lake Elementary, MI

I have to share an incredible compliment our class received today. Mrs. B., our building aide, has a variety of duties throughout the day that involve interactions with children. One of them is helping during the lunch hour. This afternoon, Mrs. B stopped at our room to share how moved she had felt by the amazing care, kindness, and respect she observed from our class.

Since the beginning of the school year, she has been noticing the many ways that children in our room look out for one another like a real family. She would hold up a lost glove near our lunch tables, and many students would respond by calling out the owner's name. When we have table-washing duties, those in charge help each other out and wait until the others are finished before they go out to recess. These are just a few acts of kindness she has shared.

Mrs. B is truly impressed with our children and the special quality of caring that is so natural and genuine to this group. Sharing this with us brought tears to her eyes, whereas hearing about it brought tears to mine and many children's.

Our class reflected on this moment and shared our realizations. We touch other people's lives, and sometimes we don't even know it. Working together and treating others with kindness brings smiles to our faces. We need to look out for each other and it's nice to know that others are looking out for us.

Our actions impact others, because we are all connected. The support, teaching, and love from home, combined with the continuous support, teaching, and love from the school family, work toward helping each child become a successful individual in our world.

What makes stories powerful is that human beings are already wired to remember them, so when concrete examples and data (as educational research and scientific discoveries) are added to a narrative, they can hold a great appeal to readers. Not only will they feel compelled to read the story but they will also be likely moved both emotionally and intellectually.

A "Student Agency" Factor

If something is personally important and relevant to students, they will "sell" it to their parents, or at least make sure that information reaches its destination. In attempts to maintain parents informed, putting students in charge of suggesting communication content might prove to be beneficial for a number of reasons. First, students communicate with their parents about school and learning. In conversations, they hear their parents' questions, doubts, or frustrations that teachers usually do not know exist. As a result, children and teens might have a better grasp on what is important to parents and what information will catch their attention.

In addition, when students are in charge of something, they want to know how what they do impacts others, so they are more likely to keep on bringing this to their parents' attention. Teachers frequently ask students to get their parents' signatures on a test or any other activity of which they want to make sure parents are aware. Often, some credit is given for delivering this signature. Although, of course, it is rather difficult to create awareness based on signatures, if there is something conceptually important to the learning process, students can be asked to make sure that their parents read the information.

There are many ways how students can become agents of awareness within their own homes and communities. It is always important to remember that they have the power to get attention from those close to them.

A "Here and Now" Factor

E-mail communication is, by far, the most preferred way for educators to share some instruction-related information. However, when it comes to creating educational awareness, it might not be as effective as schools want it to be. When a class is covering multiple ways of solving a problem in math or doing a particular project activity that parents may find unclear, for example, a lot of diligent educators reserve to sending long e-mail messages with explanations of the *what* and the *how* (and may be even the *why*) to families. Later, however, they find out that the majority of the parents have never read it. Time is wasted; frustration is high. Why would this be the case?

One frequent real-life situation is that working, education-removed parents check their e-mails on the go, often driving from work, when there is no real capacity for understanding anything lengthy or complex. At home, there are extracurricular activities, dinner, and physical exhaustion. The only time that parents might have left in their day would be spent on looking over that very classwork or homework mentioned in the e-mail. By that time, the computer is in the other room, the smart phone needs charging, and there is no desire to get up and read a long e-mail.

Meredith Copland, a second-grade teacher from Clarkston, Michigan, pairs important student work that she sends home with a sheet, providing a brief, bulleted explanation of what parents see in their child's work and the benefits of this project or learning. As expressed in a personal conversation, when she started using thinking routines in her class, Copland realized that when sent home on their own, examples of these routines meant very little to parents.

Similarly, her attempts to provide information by e-mail produced only marginal results. To create immediate relevance, she now attaches information to students' work.

This solution has a lot of merit. After the first look at a worksheet, parents are often puzzled and, therefore, motivated to find out more. Then, the attached second page supplies explanations of the routine, why it was used, and what the teacher was trying to accomplish; it also makes references to what can immediately be found in the child's work. In essence, by triggering curiosity, then conveniently satisfying it, and finally, referencing the child's work, Copland managed to help parents develop a deeper understanding of what took place at school and why such emphasis on thinking benefited their child.

A "Presence" Factor

A lot can be said about face-to-face communication. This is the time when educators have undivided attention of their audience. There is no better opportunity to establish collaboration and introduce the rationale behind classroom practices than when parents are there to listen for understanding. This is true for individual classroom meetings, grade-level gatherings, or school-wide events. Curriculum nights, therefore, present an excellent opportunity to take this first step into creating awareness not only of *what* is going to be taught in a particular grade but also of *how* it is going to be taught.

One way this can be accomplished is by showing parents a short documentary or a video featuring practices from a previous year and providing explanations of the skills children will be developing in this classroom. When physically in schools, parents tend to notice things unfamiliar to them and are likely to initiate questions leading to rich discussions. Teachers can use these questions in their future correspondence with parents to offer additional information. Since an initial inquiry has been made, parents are more willing to read what will follow.

Through conversations, teachers and administrators can determine what topics are particularly of interest to parents and supply this information through social media. It's a good time to ask parents to stay tuned to education-related social media posts (with an immediate request to follow certain Facebook pages and Twitter accounts). Even a simple request from a teacher to pay attention to what is posted will substantially increase chances of getting through.

Partnership nights have a potential to become important gatherings for establishing a shared vision of learning. Influenced by their own experiences, parents often focus on grades as outcomes of learning and admissions to good colleges as outcomes of K–12 education. However, if asked what exactly they want their children to become as a result of their time spent in a particular grade or school, parents think about their child as an individual, a citizen, and a contributor, rather than as a student.

When teachers ask parents what qualities they want their child to have at the end of a school year, regardless of a school or grade level, responses are usually very similar. Parents want their children to be not only curious, independent, confident, and creative but also kind, understanding, and empathetic. This can give start to building shared goals and connecting these goals to developing twenty-first-century dispositions through thinking, questioning and investigating, and observing and applying, rather than memorizing and testing. As a result, any subsequent information offered to parents will fall on a fertile ground and the process of creating awareness will take root.

Parent Advisory Boards (PAB) are yet another route that is used to spread awareness of important initiatives and developments in education. PAB meetings can be conducted by district or school administrators to inform parents of important instructional shifts. Parents often have a different vantage point from that of educators, so parent leaders can take the information and share it in the ways that other parents understand. The important part here, however, is to communicate to parent liaisons the expectation of sharing information within their schools and to press for group feedback at the next meeting.

A "Timing" Factor

There seems to always be hot issues in education that generate interest and stir a lot of opinionated discussions. Schools can capitalize on these topics to provide more in-depth information and to create awareness about educational trends. One of such topics, for example, is state standardized testing, especially around the time that this testing is implemented at schools. Any insights about alternative assessments, such as project-based learning and learners' portfolios, for example, could create a lot of interest in a community.

It could also be the right time to throw around ideas of what is needed for such learning or assessments to take place, including needs for technology or additional infrastructure. Often, meeting these needs becomes the community's decision in the form of tax or bond measures. To feed the right information at the right time, it is very important to stay on the top of community mood and perceptions.

The *Most Likely to Succeed* documentary, produced by Greg Whiteley and based on Tony Wagner and Ted Dintersmith's (2015) book with the same title, has made a splash in many communities. A story of a bright, fun-loving fourth grader who started failing in school and has found another way to learn brings up many ideas that are now being reconsidered in education: perseverance, worksheets and tests, real world versus traditional education, and, most importantly, what really matters in learning.

Drippings Springs ISD in Central Texas hosted three screenings of the film: one for school board members, one for every employee, and one for parents. Dr. Bruce Gearing, Dripping Springs ISD Superintendent, saw this as a way "to spark the conversation about what do we want learning to really look like, and who drives learning in the district" (as cited in Cargile, 2016, February 8, para. 5).

Although there might be various takes on the documentary itself, screenings that implore viewers to consider the human consequences of education, followed by panel discussions with teachers, superintendents, principals, and students, are powerful ways to initiate re-thinking learning within communities. Interestingly, students themselves most frequently volunteer to take lead in such projects and offer their own perspectives. Thus, the "student agency" factor is also engaged, doubling chances for generating interest in the event.

Overall, in the digital age, as the data demonstrate, "parents and non-parents alike turn to the web when they need information, and they want it now" (NSPRA, 2011, August 26, para. 4). It is the job of schools to offer reliable information to families and communities in a consistent and continuous manner.

TRY THIS

Applications for Creating Educational Communities through Communication

- Remind: This is a free application "that allows teachers to safely send text messages to parents and students regarding classroom assignments and reminders. The [application] organizes text messages by subject and allows teachers to send anything from daily affirmations to reminders about deadlines and upcoming projects."
- Buzzmob: This application "offers the ability to connect the entire community (e.g., administrators, teachers, parents and students) via a location-based platform. The [application] cuts down on paper costs by eliminating costly memos," and it connects parents to teachers.
- Class Messenger: This is a "direct, two-way messaging that . . . allows both parties to communicate about a student's potential, progress, strengths, and struggles. . . . It can be used on a phone, computer, or tablet. Parents can join a class and engage in a dialog with teachers who can send test results, reminders, photos and even videos" to parents.

- Google For Education "is a lot like Google +, except that it's for the classroom. Teachers can create a class group (similar to a Google+ Circle), create documents that can be viewed and edited by others, share information on the cloud, video chat, launch websites and share calendars." Parents can also see everything and respond.
- VolunteerSpot is an application "that helps organize group meetings, e-mails, and parent–teacher conferences." It "can be used to organize parent chaperones or school volunteers for various events, field trips, and more."
- Mailchimp is "an e-mailing service that can be tailored for educational needs. It can send automated e-mails" based on each parent's preference in communication—from one e-mail a day to multiple messages. "It allows teachers to design the layout of the e-mails and to send them anywhere, from any device."
- Edmodo is "an application with many uses. Teachers can use it to track student progress, . . . access their knowledge on a topic, export classroom data and create games based on learning standards, which can be shared with parents. It provides [educators] with easy-to-decipher charts that depict which students have surpassed their goals, which have met their goals and which have yet to meet them. Schools can . . . use Edmodo to track progress and create professional communities. The information gathered by the application can be easily shared, and students can enjoy personalized learning methods." (7 innovative apps, 2015, January 28)

Free Educational Blogs and Publications

- Mindshift: It explores the future of learning in all its dimensions, from cultural and technology trends, groundbreaking research, to education policy. The site is curated by Tina Barseghian, a journalist and mother of a grade-schooler.
- Classroom Q &A with Larry Ferlazzo (EdWeek): An English and social studies teacher at Luther Burbank High School in Sacramento, Calif., Larry Ferlazzo is the author of *Helping Students Motivate Themselves: Practical Answers To Classroom Challenges, The ESL/ELL Teacher's Survival Guide, and Building Parent Engagement In Schools.* He addresses readers' questions on classroom management, English Language Learners (ELL) instruction, lesson planning, and other issues facing teachers.
- Homeroom: Blog articles provide insights on the activities of schools, programs, grants, and other education stakeholders to promote continuing discussion of educational innovation and reform.

- ASCD inService stimulates conversation. Posts cover the biggest topics in education today and offer insight, information, and resources that empower educators to support the success of each learner.
- ASCD Express: This is a free newsletter that is delivered via e-mail every two weeks and that is filled with articles, tips, and online videos. The main topics include classroom management, differentiated instruction, formative assessment, and instructional leadership that are essential to successful educational practice.
- Getting Smart: A blog on GettingSmart.com is a community for news, stories, and leadership on innovations in learning and teaching. It is also the home of the Smart Parents blog series geared specifically to parents.
- Edutopia: This includes practical classroom strategies and tips from school practitioners, as well as lesson ideas, personal stories, and innovative approaches to improving teaching practice.
- Parent Toolkit: Produced by NBC News Education Nation, this website offers resources and tools for parents to navigate their child's journey from pre-kindergarten through high school by helping them track and support progress at each stage. It is organized by individual grade levels and offers information in four categories: Academic, Physical Development, Nutrition, and Social and Emotional Development.

Chapter 4 Snapshot: CREATING AWARENESS

FOCUS AREA	COMMON PRACTICE	WHAT TO CONSIDER
Content of Communication	Classroom-related information Organizational content Curriculum content School/district information	Learning process: an overview of assignments and topics accompanied by the associated learning behaviors Research findings in areas related to education and child development: This often explains why children are doing some specific activities or why different types of learning take place. New approaches to learning: how something is being taught and why it benefits students

(continued)

Chapter 4 Snapshot (*continued*)

FOCUS AREA	COMMON PRACTICE	WHAT TO CONSIDER
Ways of Information Delivery	Printed or electronic weekly newsletters E-mail School or district website	Social media: e.g., Facebook; Twitter; Instagram Downloadable applications: e.g., Remind, Edmodo, ClassDojo Video websites: e.g., YouTube, Vimeo, Hulu Local public television
Getting Through	Re-sending or duplicating a communication Stating importance	Telling a story Putting students in charge Offering immediate application Utilizing parents' physical presence in schools Providing the right information at the right time

Chapter Five

Seeking Engagement

Unless you try to do something beyond what you have already mastered, you will never grow.

—Ralph Waldo Emerson

Seeking Engagement is a stage when families and community members are engaged in action, as opposed to passively receiving information at the Creating Awareness stage. The word *engagement*, typically qualified by an adjective or a noun referring to parents or families, such as *parental engagement*, is somewhat overused in education. In the previous two to three decades, the term *parental engagement* was used very broadly, encompassing any type of involvement in school-located events. Although any form of parental participation in schools usually reaps some benefits, it is important to realistically assess engagement in terms of learning.

FOCUS OF ENGAGEMENT

Year after year, U.S. families, schools, and communities have been joining their efforts to create memories for children, to promote a sense of community, and to put extra cash into classrooms through various fundraisers. From teachers' perspective, working with families builds positive congenial relationships and helps obtain the much-needed funds for classrooms. It also brings parents to schools, which is always a good thing. From parents' point of view, the rationale for being involved in their children's schools is also clear. For many years, they have been told in a number of ways that children of engaged parents do better in school both academically and socially.

In comparison to many of their international counterparts, U.S. parents are, indeed, very involved. According to the *Parent and Family Involvement in Education* report (Noel, Stark, & Redford, 2015) from the National Household Education Surveys Program, in 2012, 87% of parents reported participating in a parent–teacher organization/parent–teacher association (PTO/PTA), 42% volunteered, and 58% participated in school fundraising (p. 3).

However, as cited by Amanda Ripley (2013) in her book *The Smartest Kids in the World*, data show something rather baffling: The PISA survey, given to parents of students who took this renowned international assessment in 14 countries, as well as other research within the United States uncover the same dynamics—volunteering in schools and attending events has little effect on how much children learn. Moreover, on average, children of parents who volunteered exclusively in extracurricular activities performed worse in reading than kids whose parents didn't volunteer (pp. 107–08).

Most parents realize that giving children the gift of their time and being involved in their schooling will benefit children in life. However, it seems to be commonly perceived that any type of parental involvement benefits children's education as long as it takes place in schools: Everything counts—bake sales, donuts with Mom/Dad, chaperoning field trips, and camp events. There are, certainly, many positive sides to participating in such activities, such as social, emotional, and financial benefits, but realistically speaking, such engagement has very little effect on developing critical thinking, understanding the learning process, or decoding reading material in children.

In almost all other nations, parents are not expected to volunteer or fundraise for schools. It is broadly accepted that parental involvement in student learning matters most at home. This aligns with the important role that parents play in fostering life-long learning dispositions in their children and in nurturing home learning environments that promote academic, social, and emotional growth.

Thus, the term *engagement* here implies a range of hands-on activities that necessitate some contribution of time and intellectual effort. These activities may take place not only on school grounds but also at home or any community location, and they refer to an action that is focused on shaping micro learning environments to improve student learning. Teachers and school leaders can support such ongoing engagement in a number of ways: coaching families on how to create a positive learning environment at home; inviting parents and community members to schools to witness student learning or to engage in learning of their own; and providing multiple opportunities for all stakeholders to contribute to student learning at school.

SEEING IS BELIEVING: LETTING FAMILIES IN

As a myriad of various curricular and instructional changes is currently sweeping over education, awareness alone is not enough. With the transition to the Common Core standards, for example, many parents complain about the confusing language, unnecessarily complicated ways to solve math problems, and a general lack of common sense in education. Parents were schooled at the time when there was one right way to arrive at one right answer, and without understanding the dynamics of learning and individual variations in how the brain learns, they will most likely resist this another "fad" in education. Unless parents overcome this initial reaction, it will be very difficult to create a productive learning environment at home.

Human beings gravitate toward meaningful, personally relevant experiences. The only truly effective way for families and community members to understand what goes on inside classrooms is by them stepping inside classrooms. "I have teared up on more than one occasion when I see the pride in a parent's eyes who had no idea that their maybe-difficult teenager can create a movie trailer or their shy son can do a Prezi with ease," shared Rain Chandler (2015, June 29). Parents, guardians, aunts, grandmas, friends of the family, community members—anyone who can be considered a personal cheerleader for a child—must be given an opportunity to witness this child's learning.

How to open classrooms to families seems to always be a puzzling question. There are many ways to accomplish this, ranging from student-led tours to simply allowing parents to drop in with a little advance notice. A lot has to do with the size of schools and their security, as well as with the comfort level of their staff. Nonetheless, there are options that could work for various schools.

Open Door Policy

There are a lot of teachers nationwide who are opting for an open door policy, welcoming parents to participate in classroom activities or to simply observe any time they wish. Incorporation of an open door policy helps build and strengthen trust. If schools are proud of their academic programs and teachers are proud of their students' work, they are more likely to have an open door policy.

Arne Duncan, a former U.S. Secretary of Education, sees this as a high form of accountability:

> The best way for parents to learn about the quality of public schools is by observing teachers in the classroom and seeing how the principal leads the school. Principals and teachers should make every reasonable accommodation

to show parents how their schools operate every day so that parents can make informed decisions about how to provide a high-quality education for their children. (as cited in Rotherham, 2011, March 10, para. 6)

Patricia Owens-Davis, a middle-school teacher in Memphis, Tennessee, agrees, "These should be impromptu visits that are not necessarily scripted. As an educator, I encourage my parents to drop by at any time and visit my class. The only requirement is that they stop at the office, sign in, and obtain the required visitor's badge" (as cited in Rotherham, 2011, March 10, para. 4).

An open door policy can be especially helpful to parents of children with disabilities. For instance, Variety Child Learning Center—a New York City not-for-profit center that provides special education programs for children with developmental and learning disabilities—invites parents to visit the center-based school "throughout the day without prior appointment and observe children in class and individual therapy sessions through a one-way viewing window and intercom system" (Variety Child Learning Center, n.d.).

Schools have various rules regarding an open door policy. One drawback is the constant flow of people to the school, which may distract students and teachers as well as compromise school security. For large schools, it is a good idea to schedule visits so that classrooms aren't overcrowded with visitors, interfering with instruction. For other schools, selecting a daily time window or specific days and times for observations works just as well. School leaders, however, have to keep in mind that the projected attitude of the first school staff member whom the visitor encounters sets the stage for his or her perception of the school. Parents become wary of schools that are unfriendly or that make visitations difficult.

Open Classroom Events

For students, open classroom events are an occasion to show off their work. For their families, these events present an opportunity to get snapshots of children's learning and to absorb the atmosphere of the classroom learning environment that could be later re-created at home. It is good to invite families for a visit after a month or two into a school year. A teacher usually decides on what aspects of student learning parents need to focus on during the visit and what understandings they need to reach. Most commonly, the main reasons for bringing parents in are to observe a different type of instruction, to experience a classroom learning environment, and to understand new-to-them methodology (see Textbox 5.1).

Textbox 5.1

COME AND LEARN WITH US!—OPEN CLASSROOM EVENT

Meredith Copland, Second-Grade Teacher,

Bailey Lake Elementary, MI

Shortly after their winter break, I asked students to invite their parents for an hour of learning. Since both, children and I, wanted parents to understand the thinking routines used in our classrooms, students wrote invitations using the *Claim Support Question* thinking routine to present their parents with a personal, compelling reason to attend the event. For example, one child wrote this:

Dear Mom and Dad,
    Claim: You should come and see how we think and learn in room 13!
    Support: Because we do amazing things! You will love it and it will be fun!
    Question: Do you want to see how I learn with my classmates?

Children were in charge of delivering invitations and making sure that their parents RSVP. Parents also completed the *Think Puzzle Explore* routine to assess their prior knowledge of cultures of thinking—our learning framework. A lot of them admitted that they knew very little about it and were intrigued to learn how it related to the curriculum. It became clear that e-mails couldn't satisfy all of the parental curiosity; to truly understand, parents had to see it for themselves.

During our open classroom event, students took parents on a walking tour of the classroom and hallway, where we displayed examples of various visible thinking routines completed by children. They gave a brief explanation of each routine and answered all of the adults' questions. Later, parents observed as the students engaged in book discussions guided by a *Micro Lab Protocol*, followed by a whole class *Number Talk* session.

We asked parents to join students in the *Chalk Talk* routine, featuring math equations similar to those covered in the Number Talk. Parents and children worked together side by side, observing each other's solutions and learning from each other. This was a powerful sight to witness.

After an hour of learning, parents reflected on their experience by completing the *I Used to Think Now I Think* thinking routine to evaluate their observations. It was evident that many of them had experienced a shift in perceptions of both learning/teaching practices and their children's abilities.

After the first open classroom event, I received many e-mails from class parents, reiterating their gratitude for the opportunity to experience learning with their children and to gain an understanding of the learning processes and practices. These e-mails and conversations with families cemented my conviction that letting parents witness their children while they are thinking, making connections, and applying what they know in the learning process does more for achieving supportive and consistent learning environments at homes than any other strategy.

Community Visits

Though similar to open classroom events, community visits are open to anyone who wishes to learn more about current educational practices and go to classrooms to see how students experience education. These visits are planned well in advance and are offered as frequently as schools' schedules can accommodate them. Community visits usually last two to three hours to include activities and short observations in several classrooms. There is a lot of flexibility in what schools can showcase during these visits, but an introductory activity, classroom observations, and a follow-up discussion with teachers and principals typically make up the itinerary.

Community visits present an invaluable opportunity to bring community decision makers and business owners to schools. Their firsthand experiences with student learning could make it easier to elevate school–community connections to collaborative partnerships. To make the most of these visits, direct invitations should be sent to targeted community members; whereas families and the community at large can be invited through e-mail blasts and social media posts (see Textbox 5.2).

Textbox 5.2

COMMUNITY VISITS

Glenn Gualtieri, Principal,

Bailey Lake Elementary, MI

At our school, where there is a culture in which all involved grow in their thinking, we strive to have families and community members be partners in the learning process. We aim at not only having parents know their child's story of learning but also having them grow and enhance their thinking through the school experience. With each school culture and administrative style of leading being unique, a thread of engagement can drive parent and community participation. It is necessary for families and the extended community to experience the learning, language and environment for learning that occurs in school.

Our school invited families and community members to spend two to three hours one morning emerging in the type of learning that students experienced during the day. After the initial explanation of ideas in a short presentation by the principal, attendees had an opportunity to see examples of student thinking displayed in the halls and to visit a fourth-grade classroom to observe young scientists reasoning and collaborating while writing headlines about electricity.

After this observation, we engaged participants in some hands-on activities, leading them to a deeper level of thinking and understanding. This event allowed us to accomplish two things: to provide families and community members with information on the latest instructional practices at our school and to gain a better perspective on how to support children's learning at home or other community locations.

LEARNING, TRAINING, AND COACHING

Regardless of diplomas or degrees that parents hold, knowing how to support their children's learning at home often requires some basic training in methodology, learning-related concepts, and frameworks practiced in their children's schools. There is a need, therefore, to offer hands-on learning opportunities to parents beyond what a single teacher can do within one particular classroom. Without such training, creating a coherent learning environment at home is a nearly impossible task.

Schools that are tuned to families do schedule a few parent learning events throughout a school year, but usually randomly, without any systematic approach. Although these events are beneficial, they only cover a small portion of what is typically needed. Schools and school districts have to assess which specific areas of student learning are in need of clarification or "demystification" and develop a learning plan for parents and community members—a series of learning events. Parent learning opportunities can be offered at school, district, and community levels.

Fishbowl Learning Sessions

One powerful way to involve adults in student learning is fishbowl learning—an effective strategy that is used in many settings when an in-depth discussion of a specific topic is desired. Since fishbowl learning is focused on how a group of people can work together effectively, it often helps build a shared vision and understanding. Fishbowl learning can take place during open classroom or school events or as separate sessions that are aimed at providing families and community members with an understanding of subject-related instructional practices or the learning process.

Students usually model how they collaborate to construct meaning from a text or make sense of a specific math problem, for example. Parents are invited to view a lesson to experience the dialog, shared thinking, and learning thread. This way, they become firsthand witnesses to this particular learning. After students (usually sitting in a circle) finish their discussions, parents (usually sitting in the outside circle) share their thoughts about what they observed.

This discussion can be focused on various skills, methodology, or other aspects of learning. Depending on the age of students, a teacher or administrator might invite parents to add their thoughts on the subject of the fishbowl conversation and give students time to respond to them. A parent–student discussion about what is being learned brings a lot of insight to all—educators, students, and parents.

Book Clubs and Parent Libraries Centered on Learning

Education-centered libraries are a good way to offer parents books on education and education-related topics that connect to a district vision. Lakeview Elementary School in Hoffman Estates, Illinois, serving nearly 550 students from kindergarten through sixth grade, offers a parent lending library right in their school building. There are two ways that parents can borrow a book: stop by the main office and sign out a title that interests them or view a list of titles online and send in the book request form with their children. The books are sent home in a child's backpack and returned to school the same way within a two-week period.

The books offered by the school include titles on "ADHD, anger, autism, bullying, college, death, discipline, divorce, friendship, homework, internet safety, self esteem, social skills, and much more" (Lakeview Elementary School, n.d.). Libraries could be limited to one school's families or open to the entire community. In areas with lower levels of education among their population, promotion of literacy and education awareness to families is of great value.

In Santa Monica, California, A World is Just a Book Away (WIJABA) organization opened 26 parent libraries to help address requests made by parents "who would drop off their children at school and then wait until the children have finished school to take them home. These libraries provide an opportunity for parents to expand their own knowledge and serve as reminders of the importance of education" (WIJABA, n.d., para. 2). In a parent library, there is a collection of at least 50 books that are handpicked by local parents and include anything from traditional cooking recipes to sustainable agriculture to creative parenting advice.

Book clubs facilitated by educators are another way to engage parents in learning. Books could be selected based on the needs of particular schools or districts and include the latest educational research and effective practices. When parents read about and discuss educational ideas, the level of learning support at home is likely to increase.

Training and Instruction

In any school, opportunities can be created for parents to experience the language, environment, and approach to learning through a number of strategically scheduled, coherent events throughout the year. They include parental workshops, booster meetings, and informational nights.

Parental Workshops with an Emphasis on Learning

Parental workshops are a series of trainings that equip families with knowledge and skills to act in various learning-related situations involving their children. Workshops can help parents understand different educational concepts, such as college readiness or the Common Core standards, or target social and emotional learning and discipline. For instance, if a school is learning the theory and practice of the Love and Logic approach to managing student behavior, or the Leader in Me approach for the education of character, or the mindfulness to nurture student sense of well-being, families and community members have to be included in this learning. In addition to monthly tips in a school newsletter, a series of learning sessions should be arranged throughout a year.

Booster Meetings

Booster meetings usually afford parents some support in a particular subject. They are focused on subject-specific learning strategies and methodology, which usually strengthens a learning environment at home. Booster meetings frequently target literacy, math, special education, or accelerated programs. They provide an environment in which attendees can acquire knowledge and skills as well as deepen their understanding of a subject. Judy Bradbury and Susan Busch (2015), authors of *Empowering Families*, suggest that to support ongoing involvement, effective strategies, practical how-to's, common language, and a variety of accessible suggestions should be shared during these periodic meetings.

Parent Nights

Parent data night is one example of parent nights that schools can hold for their families. This is an event that offers families and community members an opportunity to ask questions regarding student learning data and what they can do to help their child progress. Although most parents are used to seeing report cards, very few of them can actually "decode" these reports in terms of learning. Since schools might use various systems to measure student progress, information about assessments and what they measure is vital.

Maureen Holt, a Title I teacher and reading specialist from Humboldt Elementary School in a rural area of Arizona, holds parent data nights to meet individually with each parent to go over the reports. She uses this time to explain acronyms and scores, to pinpoint areas in which the child had problems, and to supply tips and tricks for providing help at home (Humboldt Elementary, 2015, April 7). School-wide parent data nights can be scheduled a few times per year to go over testing objectives, methodology, and scoring. These meetings are also good opportunities to discuss learning feedback documents and how to understand them.

During parent nights, or any other after-school training for parents, the provision of childcare might substantially increase participation. There are usually some resources in any school district that could be used to make this happen, especially if all of the workshops and meetings are scheduled ahead of time. High schools have leadership programs and Honor Society students who are in need of community service hours. They can earn these hours by volunteering to watch younger students. Girl scouts and community service-oriented clubs might also become good resources for schools when they need to provide childcare.

LEARNING FEEDBACK

To be partners in education, parents must have a good grasp on their children's learning. Traditionally, apart from short parent–teacher conferences, which many parents of secondary students tend to ignore, report cards have been the only official feedback on student learning that parents saw in their homes. Since states adopted their own content and learning standards for each grade, a growing number of schools have been developing standards-based report cards in hopes that they will keep parents informed about their students' progression toward the standards. Instead of usual letter grades, marks that indicate mastery of the skills are frequently used. As school districts are working toward more meaningful learning feedback, there are few things to be taken into consideration.

Report Cards and Documents

Many district leaders see the purpose of learning feedback in providing parents (and learners) with the understanding of a child's learning progress—that is, where a child stands in his or her advancement toward mastery of a particular standard. However, this should only be a start. Parents, as partners in education of their children, have to be expected to take action based on this information. Thus, consideration has to be given to the action that a learning feedback document should inspire in parents. If district and school administrators entertain this idea, their reporting documents can become significantly more telling.

Ideally, parents need to understand their children's progress to help them improve their learning and to motivate them to excel further. This means that a report card or document should provide clear evidence of a student's growth and offer some indicators of where a child stands at this time in his or her journey toward the standard mastery expectations. In other words, if a standard is expected to be mastered by the end of April, in February, parents need to know whether a child is making a sufficient progress to meet this goal, has already reached it and requires something more challenging, or needs help. To accomplish this, learning feedback should:

- Limit a number of categories for each standard. An overwhelming amount of information makes it very difficult for parents to understand their child's overall performance in mastering a standard; so, three to four categories for each standard should be sufficient.
- Show a child's progression in mastering the same part of a standard from the day it was first introduced and assessed to the point when the document was created; this might mean a few marks for each standard's category in each report card or a simple continuum graphic with hash marks.
- Provide occasional longitudinal reporting—a progression measured in reverse from the mastery of a standard; this is a prediction of whether a student will get this mastery on time and whether a child is progressing at a good rate.
- Provide a benchmark for individual growth—a judgment about whether a student's current performance aligns with expectations for that particular student at that time. If a student is near a standard's mastery in October, the expectation for this student might be achieving the state of mastery by January, not April.
- Differentiate between proficiency and mastery. It should indicate how a student who has achieved proficiency can grow further.

It is rather difficult to create one document that can provide all of this information. Therefore, a learning feedback system, continuously supplying parents with a comprehensive picture of their children's learning growth, should be developed. This could be accomplished via learning portfolios that are put together by learners and teachers and that accompany a report card. Online reporting systems that many school districts use to post student schedules, attendance, and grades could be utilized to keep parents aware of their child's progress as well. If handled correctly, parent–teacher conferences can also become a great occasion for parents and teachers to talk about a student's learning journey.

Twenty-First-Century Conferences

While sharing a student's learning story, teachers let parents see an artifact and hear how their child has grown as a learner, a person, and a contributor. This artifact, i.e., evidence of learning, could be an essay, a project portfolio, a digital presentation, lab documentation, or anything that represents learning. Sharing stories about students as learners is very important. Each learning story should highlight the strengths and challenges as seen through the lens of a student's samples.

Conferences are also the time for parents to tell teachers about their child. Teachers have to give parents a chance to ask questions and to add to the story by sharing insights about their child. For best impact, teachers need to send questions to the home prior to conferences and then take the lead in asking for the information. Alternative sitting arrangements with no barriers, such as comfortable chairs in a circle, immediately change the dynamics of the conversation.

Student-led parent conferences are now becoming popular in schools. This format puts students in charge of assessing their learning and of explaining it to parents. Throughout the year, students set goals and collect work that represents their learning. During a conference, they show the artifacts to parents and explain class objectives. The role of a teacher changes from being the leader of the conference to a facilitator, whereas students move from being non-participants to leaders.

Mary Tedrow, a director of the Shenandoah Writing Project at Shenandoah University and the Porterfield Endowed English Chair at John Handley High School in Virginia, sees a great power behind these conferences not only in explaining their student's progress to parents but also in forming their link to the school, modeling discussions about school, and demystifying what goes on in the classroom.

> The first year my students presented their work to a parent, there was a palpable change in the climate of the room. Making the home-school connection immediately created a less threatening learning environment. Because the parents had a clear idea of what was happening during the day, presentation night extended the discussions at home. For our large projects, all parents began asking questions at home and assisting with resources. (as cited in Ferlazzo, 2016, January 23)

Families usually do become more engaged in discussions with their children than with teachers. However, there are also some reservations. Often, the conference may be a parent's only opportunity to share with the teacher confidential information that the student doesn't need to hear. Perhaps one-on-one meetings with parents to share their personal concerns could be incorporated throughout a year.

CREATING LEARNING SYSTEMS

A growing number of school districts are beginning to realize that education of parents, caregivers, and communities, in general, especially in the areas with many adversity factors, is just as important as education of students. Thus, virtual spaces, where families and communities can engage in various classes and take part in discussions with teachers and other parents, are now offered by many districts. Virtual platforms are good for individual engagement in learning as well as for social engagement and support. They enable schools to include all family members into learning and to extend it to the entire community.

However, the most advanced level of learning that schools and districts (often in collaboration with other learning or community organizations) can offer to families is through systemic, coherent, and supportive learning structures that respond to the needs of a community. These systems are usually multi-focused, as opposed to parental workshops or booster meetings that are typically centered around one topic or subject. In addition to online support and resources, they incorporate frequent, regularly scheduled meetings and may lead to earning certifications. Parent academies and parent universities are two examples of such systems.

Parent Academies

Parent academies are small educational institutions within educational institutions that provide continuous learning and coaching opportunities to families and community members. Parent academies combine a variety of resources that appeal to lifestyles and needs of various families. They offer face-to-face or online coaching, run informational meetings on important educational concepts and policies, and provide an online help desk or assistance with school-related issues.

Guilford County in North Carolina, for example, has created a comprehensive model for coaching parents through workshops, videos, and online tutoring free of charge—the Guilford Parent Academy. The academy provides information and training on a variety of topics for parents, grandparents, and family members and is designed to assist them as they help their students succeed at school and in life.

Since many parents, interested in attending face-to-face informational sessions, had other obligations, evening hours did not always work. To solve this problem, the Guilford County district partnered with companies that employed many parents in their community to run the workshops onsite during employees' lunch or dinner breaks (Pierce, 2016, January 24). These partnerships allowed schools to overcome one of the major barriers to parental engagement: a lack of time.

Parent Universities

A parent university is an even larger undertaking than a parent academy. It is usually a joint initiative between a community and a school district that is aimed at helping parents become full partners in their children's education. Parent universities offer free courses in a structured fashion, similar to higher education establishments, and various family activities. At the end, there is always an opportunity for participants to earn certificates and even become leaders in parental education.

At Charlotte-Mecklenburg Schools in North Carolina, the parent university offers workshops in schools, public libraries, YMCAs, houses of worship, businesses, and other community locations. More than 70 course topics are available for families, with workshops "ranging from topics like Helping Your Child Prepare for the End-of-Grade and End-of-Course Tests, to Preparing for Kindergarten, Middle and High School, to Surviving Adolescence" (Charlotte-Mecklenburg Schools, n.d.).

When in 2014, Detroit Public Schools in Michigan opened their parent university—a semester of coursework that allowed family members to earn certifications—Jack Martin, emergency manager, Detroit Public Schools, saw the goal of this university in educating and empowering parents "as partners, advocates and lifelong teachers in their child's education by providing them with educational courses and leadership opportunities" (as cited in Detroit Public Schools, 2014, February 12, para. 3). Parents and community members could choose from 20 free classes offered in eight Parent Resource Centers. The development of a professional curriculum for parents was tailored to the district's population.

There were four tracks offered within this program:

- Student success: Helping children of all ages
- Life skills: Maximizing your potential
- Parenting: Effectively raising children
- Leadership: Inspiring others with a vision

The four certificates included Parent Leader Certificate, Parent Educator Certificate, Parent Mentor Certificate, and Parent Advocate Certificate. To graduate, participants had to complete 10 classes during the semester, two classes from each track. Initially, registration was limited to the first 150 parents who applied, but the university is looking to expand its capacity (Detroit Public Schools, 2014, February 12).

Another Michigan-based parent university in Grand Rapids Public Schools district also provides courses free of charge to all district parents and community members in four areas of focus: Effective Parenting, Personal Growth and Development, Navigating the Educational System, and Health and Wellness. Courses use a research-based curriculum, define a skill or enhance awareness that students take away from their experience, and relate to the needs of families (Parent University, n.d.).

PROFESSIONAL, SOCIAL, AND HUMAN CAPITAL

Over the years, contemporary economists have been noticing one persistent trend: Individuals consciously invest in themselves to improve their own personal economic returns, and most commonly, they do so through education (Keeley, 2007, p. 31). Human capital—people—is a driving force behind the economic growth of any country, company, or organization. Thus, to grow and prosper, school systems, too, have to capitalize on their human capital, which includes family and community members.

As human beings with diverse interests, all parents are experts in something. Moreover, most parents view an improvement in the education of their children as investing in themselves, as it yields real returns: improvements in their family's well-being. Therefore, inviting families to share their expertise with students can serve a double purpose: enhance student learning and communicate to parents that their expertise and investment matter to schools.

Classroom Instruction Contributors

Children learn best when they can see and experience practical applications of what is being taught. Even best schools cannot have all of the resources to make this happen. Using parental expertise in a classroom is not a complicated task, and it can greatly benefit children, teachers, and families. A teacher can identify special talents, skills, or knowledge of class parents with a simple questionnaire at the beginning of a school year.

Based on this information, educators or grade-level teams can match every parent with at least one subject's unit of study or an activity that is planned for the school year. A parent can be contacted, well in advance, with a request to teach a mini-lesson, demonstrate an experiment, lead an activity or a workshop, or do anything else that enhances student learning.

If one of class parents is a biologist or an electrical engineer, for example, he or she can come for a demonstration during a science block. A parent–builder can lead a math activity requiring construction according to specific parameters. In a lesson about planetary systems, a parent–astronomer can make this science topic real to students. While writing poetry or a personal narrative, students may be inspired by a parent who has published a book.

Parents who come from other countries and cultures can make a unit on culture relevant and meaningful to students. No matter what they do, singling parents out for their skills and asking them to be part of the instructional process at school sends a powerful message that parents are respected and valued. Students feel proud to see their parents as teachers; educators get invaluable free resources for nearly all their needs; and, more importantly, parents, teachers, and students learn from each other.

Learning Leaders and Liaisons

Parents know better than school administrators about how to reach other parents and to explain things in ways that they can understand and find engaging. It is not by accident that parent academies and parent universities heavily rely on parent leaders to coordinate and run courses, workshops, online help, and other activities related to adult learning. Parent universities frequently provide opportunities for their graduates to become trained parent university instructors and place them into internships with partner agencies.

If parent universities are not an option, there are other ways to tap into parental intellectual resources. Guilford County district, for example, employs a team of "parent liaisons" to help educate the parental community about its various programs. These parent volunteers are considered an extension of the office. As school districts might not be able to readily find volunteers who can take a lot of time from their hectic schedules, Guilford County offers parent liaisons a small cash incentive of up to $150 per month in exchange for their time (Pierce, 2016, January 24), and even this small monetary reward makes a difference.

One way or the other, schools can drastically enhance a macro learning environment of their students if they make parents and community members feel welcome at school, provide them with multiple opportunities to learn and contribute, and utilize human capital of the entire community.

REFLECT ON THIS

For Teachers and Principals

1. What does family and community engagement look like in my district, school, or classroom? Is it centered on learning?
2. How much time do I spend on working with families and members of the community on student learning (not just responding or troubleshooting)? How can I build in time to do so on a regular basis?
3. Am I truly open to letting families and community members in my school or classroom to observe and participate in student learning? Do I solicit honest feedback?
4. If I were to open my school or classroom to families, what would be my first step?

5. What are the most challenging areas for families in the current instruction and assessments in my school or classroom? What learning opportunities can I provide to them?
6. Do I or my teachers offer parents regular (at least monthly) updates on their students' learning progress in a particular subject? How can I make this happen?
7. What is the goal of my or my school's teacher–parent conferences? What documentation do we have during conferences to show a student's growth?
8. What is one thing that I can do tomorrow to engage families in learning?

For District Administrators

1. What learning opportunities for families and community members exist in my district on a regular basis? Do I consider this important?
2. What are my district families' main challenges in understanding student learning and district needs to support this learning?
3. What can I do to provide consistent, ongoing learning and support to my families and the community? How do I determine what the needs may be?
4. Do I value professional and human capital of families and community members enough to include them in student instruction or allow them to coach students, other parents, or staff?
5. What are the factors that separate schools and families in my district? What could be the first step to removing these separators?
6. What is one thing that I can do tomorrow to engage families and the community in learning?

Chapter 5 Snapshot: SEEKING ENGAGEMENT

FOCUS AREA	COMMON PRACTICE	WHAT TO CONSIDER
Scope of Engagement	Volunteering in extracurricular activities Helping in classrooms Running fundraisers Organizing parties Chaperoning field trips	Obtaining knowledge and supporting student learning Tending to a child's learning and providing a nurturing learning environment at home Witnessing student learning and/or engaging in own learning Contributing to instruction and parental learning
Letting Families in	Curriculum nights Parent–teacher conferences Class parties Extracurricular events	Open door policy Open classroom events Community visits Partnership nights

(continued)

Chapter 5 Snapshot (*continued*)

FOCUS AREA	COMMON PRACTICE	WHAT TO CONSIDER
Learning Feedback	Grade-based report cards Performance-centered parent–teacher conferences Test results	Student portfolios Learning progress-centered parent–teacher conferences Student self-assessments Standards-based reports with personalized feedback
Learning Systems	Learning systems for educating children	Learning systems for educating families Learning-specific training and coaching through various workshops, booster meetings, learning sessions, and presentations Parent academies and universities Family centers

Chapter Six

Supporting Collaboration

We need to develop and disseminate an entirely new paradigm and practice of collaboration that supersedes the traditional silos that have divided governments, philanthropies and private enterprises for decades and replace it with networks of partnerships working together to create a globally prosperous society.

—Simon Mainwaring

Supporting Collaboration is a stage when partnerships are enabled and sustained. As families, community organizations and agencies, and other stakeholders gain understanding of learning and what it takes to support it, they also gain insight into schools' needs to successfully provide important educational opportunities to all students. At this stage, schools enter various collaborations with families, parental and community organizations, and other learning institutions, whereas relationships among all of the partners are distinctly collegial (i.e., based on mutual ownership and shared responsibility for decision making.). There is sharing of power, resources, and goals. Often, this stage starts with re-designing habitual ways in which districts and schools operate and govern.

INSTITUTIONALIZATION AND POLICIES

School districts that are serious about family and community partnerships around student learning are coming to realize that these initiatives require a serious commitment of resources: development of staff, hiring a family–community coordinator with a clear set of responsibilities, investing in growing parent leaders, and expanding infrastructure. More importantly, however, to stabilize this new educational culture and to ensure its longevity, it is necessary to make it officially documented and embedded in practices, policies, and operations of the school or district.

In 2013, California Governor Jerry Brown signed the *Local Control Funding Formula* (LCFF) into law. Not only did this make parent engagement one of the eight statewide education priorities but it also elevated it to a legal requirement. The *Local Control Funding Formula* gave California school districts an opportunity to direct energy and resources into institutionalizing home–school partnerships by making this work an integral part of district operations. The state also developed the *Local Control Accountability Plan* and evaluation rubrics, which were intended to help parents hold districts accountable for delivering on their commitment to the students and families that they serve.

> It is about having honest conversations, embracing different points of view, and providing foundational supports to sustain change over the long haul. At its core, it is about building relationships. It is about building the "Four Cs"— Capabilities, Connections, Cognition and Competence—in both parents and school staff, so that everyone is prepared to move forward together to create the conditions and systems that enable all children to fulfill their potential. It is about learning together. (Mapp, 2015, p. 3)

With this new law's requirement of districts to present clear evidence of how they are attempting to create powerful partnerships between educators and families, schools can no longer go through compliance motions of the past; rather, "they have to move towards authentic, outcome-based parent engagement programs, and to adopt a measurement system to track their progress" (Families in Schools, 2015, p. 4). When building partnerships with families and the community becomes a planned, documented effort with measurable deliverables, it integrates into the school system not as an afterthought, but as an educational priority.

Whether a state legally requires this or not, it is necessary for district leaders and school boards of educations to institutionalize changes that integrate families and communities in the education of students. *Institutionalization* can be defined as "systematic efforts to stabilize a successful innovation for the long term [. . .] The innovation gets written into the DNA of the school—into the mission statement, communications to students and parents, formal documents that describe the school's teaching and learning commitments, hiring practices for new teachers and even new principals, and staff positions . . . " (Perkins & Reese, 2014, p. 46). Although districts do have different needs, there are some areas that have to be considered by all of them.

Mission Statement

School and district mission statements reflect the direction where schools are going in educating students, as well as how and with whom they are going there. Mission statements reflect the most important goals and beliefs that school districts have about students, their learning and needs for the future. Incorporation of the co-creators of learning environments in mission statements makes a powerful statement that families and communities are indeed full-rights partners in education. A few examples of such mission statements come from different districts across the United States:

- Michigan: "In partnership with parents and community, the mission of the NCSD is to ensure that all students develop the knowledge, skills, and character necessary to achieve their highest potential and to be productive members of an ever changing global society" (Novi Community Schools, n.d.).
- Virginia: "The Virginia Beach City Public Schools, in partnership with the entire community, will empower every student to become a life-long learner who is a responsible, productive and engaged citizen within the global community" (Virginia Beach City Public Schools, n.d.).
- South Dakota: "The Harrisburg School District optimizes student potential through the pursuit of educational excellence in partnership with the school community" (Harrisburg School District, n.d.).
- California: "The mission of the Brea Olinda Unified School District, in partnership with home and community, is to provide all students a quality education that prepares and inspires them to strive for high goals, become responsible, contributing citizens, and continue learning all their lives" (Brea Olinda Unified School District, n.d.).
- Texas: "Katy Independent School District, the leader in educational excellence, together with family and community, provides unparalleled learning experiences designed to prepare and inspire each student to live an honorable, fulfilling life . . . *to create the future*" (Katy Independent School District, n.d.).

Good mission statements are more than just words that get forgotten as soon as they are officially adopted as a mission. Statements that have little practical meaning are often not supported by practice. Thus, it is necessary to ensure that specific goals, expectations, reporting, learning, and accountability for family and community collaboration are reflected in a district's strategic plan.

Strategic Plan

A strategic plan sets forth what a district aims to achieve, how it will achieve it, and how it will know whether it has achieved it. New York–based East Syracuse Minoa (EMS) Central School District is on a mission to "prepare students for the 21st Century by engaging all learners in meaningful learning experiences that meet the highest educational and ethical standards in a caring, collaborative learning community supported through partnerships with parents and families, businesses, civic organizations, and higher education" (East Syracuse Minoa Schools, n.d., p. 2). To support the mission of creating a learning community through partnerships with various stakeholders, district administrators made this collaboration central to developing the district's strategic plan:

> The ESM Strategic Plan for 2013-2018 was created through the strong collaboration and synergy of District staff, parents, community members, business and higher education partners, and our students, who reflected on our first Strategic Plan, and en-visioned the experiences our students need to develop the knowledge and skills to be prepared for college and career, and excel in their future. (p. 4) (see Textbox 6.1)

Policies and Operational Procedures

A strategic plan sets forth a direction and goals, whereas school or district policies make achieving these goals possible. Consequently, it is often necessary to take stock of existing policies and to re-evaluate them according to what the strategic plan aspires to accomplish. This can be done by revising existing policies or adopting new policies that address school–family–community partnerships and responsibilities of all partners for student learning.

- Classroom supplemental instruction policy outlines use of external expertise (of parents or community members) on a repetitive basis to enhance or differentiate classroom instruction. For students who are excelling in writing or math, for example, advanced workshops in these subjects, run by an outside expert during normal school hours, might be a good way to ensure that each student learns according to his or her speed.
- After-school instruction policy encourages after-school curriculum-related instruction. Often, after-school clubs and activities that promote academic learning are run by educators, whereas parents or organizations organize clubs that are centered on extracurricular activities. Policies that enable community members and organizations to offer their academic services (e.g., tutoring or subject-specific enrichment) on school grounds might prove to be effective in creating powerful learning environments.

Textbox 6.1

EAST SYRACUSE MINOA CENTRAL SCHOOL DISTRICT, NEW YORK

Strategic Plan, 2013–18

Goal 2 of this Strategic Plan, *Building Capacity and Sustaining Relationships to Increase Student Learning Outcome*, clearly states that the focus of partnerships is on learning: "relationships within and beyond the school community will be supported and sustained to maximize learning for all students" (East Syracuse Minoa Schools, n.d., p. 10). Student and adult expectations are specified and clearly correspond with one another.

STUDENT EXPECTATIONS

- Build and sustain healthy relationships with students, parents, peers and the community.
- Demonstrate an understanding and application of leadership skills.
- Actively engage in learning with one's family throughout their educational experience/process.
- Show evidence of learning and participation with business and community partners both within and beyond the school community/building.

ADULT EXPECTATIONS

- Build and sustain relationships with students, parents, peers, and the community.
- Develop the leadership capacity of students and adults.
- Foster a culture for active family engagement throughout an educational process.
- Enhance community and business partnerships to provide expertise and authentic learning opportunities for students and staff for career awareness and development (p. 11).

By 2018, the district is expecting to see concrete results, aligning expected results to the following indicators of success:

- All schools will implement a system-wide process for a 100% Personal Learning Plan (PLP)—100% of students will create, monitor, and reflect on two or more annual goals for their PLP to increase student learning.
- All students will participate in at least one service—100% of students will participate in at least one learning opportunity annually and will write a reflection as a part of their PLP.
- All families are informed and empowered to adopt the roles and strategies that have been proven to positively impact student achievement—100% of families will engage in supporting their child's learning.
- All students will communicate and/or collaborate with the community, business and/or education partners on an annual basis—100% of students will participate in a collaborative learning opportunity with the community, business and/ or education partners and will write a reflection as a part of their PLP (p. 12).

- Alternative instructional locations (e.g., apprentice workshops) policies approve use of specific community facilities and their internal instructors as extensions of students' classrooms. Curriculum-related instruction and on-the-job training can be simultaneously provided by businesses or community organizations at their own locations. Credits issued by these entities should be counted toward students' graduation requirements.
- Internships policies give local organizations the power to train students during summer months and to allow them to receive credit toward graduation.
- "Other enrollment" policies pre-approve collaborations with other learning organizations, such as community colleges and universities, to provide off-site learning opportunities.

From an operational standpoint, there are always questions of funding and responsibilities. Finding or re-allocating funds is not an easy process, but it is possible with proper planning. In Boston Public Schools, Thomas Payzant, a former district superintendent and recipient of the Broad Prize for Urban Education, embarked on creating a new system for family and community engagement by withdrawing funds from some other parent-related programs to invest into central organizational structure and parent information centers.

In terms of responsibility, the original plan called for creating teams in student services in individual schools that would be reporting to deputy superintendents. Payzant, however, chose to enact a different plan, which was proposed by community members. He created a separate Office of Family and Community Engagement, led by a deputy superintendent reporting directly to him. A few years later, again with input from families and community members, Boston Public Schools began the Family and Community Outreach Coordinators Pilot Initiative to bring consistency in how various schools partnered with families.

There are two main lessons that came with this experience:

- School districts must co-construct a family and community engagement strategy with parents and community members and listen to their voices.
- School districts should make evaluation and accountability a key component of their family and community engagement plan (Weiss & Westmoreland, 2006).

Professional Development

Presence of partnership-centered programs is not the only factor that expands district capacity for forming partnerships with families and communities. Just as important is the palatable presence at all leadership levels of the eight cultural forces (Ritchhart, 2015) that shape a culture of partnerships. The mindset of partnerships is not something that can be achieved overnight; it calls for staff professional development on building and sustaining family–community partnerships.

"Districts and schools have to train teachers, school staff and administrators to understand and practice quality parent engagement, recognizing that it requires a series of skills that can be improved with practice and strong coaching" (Families in Schools, 2015, p. 5). Administrators and educators must work with each other to share experiences of opening their schools to families and to brainstorm opportunities for fostering a rich macro learning environment in their community.

Keeping developing partnerships transparent and visible to all stakeholders is vital. After making families and the public aware of the partnerships initiative launched by the district, it is important to keep stakeholders aware of the progress as well. Updates can be delivered in various forms:

- Electronic monthly or quarterly reports
- Student work, developed in collaboration with families or community organizations, displayed on schools' websites and bulletin boards
- Visible presence and acknowledgment of community partners and representatives of parental organizations at major school and district functions
- Stories of successful partnership initiatives and practices shared on school and district social media

Schools should also consider including parent or community leaders in staff professional development on family–school–community partnerships. Such allied training will help develop personal connections and shared understanding, which enables various stakeholders to work together as partners.

RE-THINKING COLLABORATION

For many years, most members of local communities have been very removed from K–12 education. Parent-driven organizations, commonly known as parent–teacher associations (PTAs) and parent–teacher organizations (PTOs), were predominantly the only "outsiders" allowed to play some role in the work of schools, but even their efforts were frequently focused on fundraising, organizing extracurricular events, and recruiting volunteers to help with class parties or other needs.

Presently, school and district leaders have an option and an opportunity to re-envision partnerships with families and communities—from designing new ways in which schools and educators interact with parents on a day-to-day basis to restructuring how school and district officials collaborate with parental and community organizations. The first thing that needs to be considered is the concept of collaboration.

Re-evaluating Assumptions

Educators, parents, and community members represent very different groups in relation to the system of education. As members of these groups, they are embedded in networks of friends and co-workers, absorbing their emotions and being influenced by their dispositions. Drawing from their recent research on a range of interdisciplinary networks, Lamont, Boix Mansilla, and Sato (2016, May 3) suggest that "meaningful personal relations, which are at once interactive and emotional, fuel the construction of a climate of conviviality, openness to new relationships, and the trust perceived as necessary for cognitively fertile collaboration" (para. 8). This means that collaborators are inclined to put in effort, largely because they enjoy the sense of belonging and trust that exists in collaborative groups.

In recent years, a number of school and district leaders have been creating collaborative groups with parents and community organizations to work on specific initiatives or to solicit advice. However, these efforts often don't deliver expected results, because "unspoken" assumptions (i.e., mental models) that educational systems have about partnering with families and communities don't promote this sense of belonging and trust.

Group meetings are usually held at schools, on the same weekday each month, and serve as an informational exchange between a principal/superintendent and other parties. Schools generally determine what roles their partners are going to play or how parents should be engaged, often limiting their roles to delivering funds, chaperoning, or providing some sort of assistance. Most decisions are handed down, and there is the unspoken assumption that schools know best and families and community members just have to listen and "collaborate."

School leaders and staff have to deliberately work on creating new mental models that come with the mindset of partnerships. When Teaching for Change, for example, launched the Tellin' Stories parent-engagement initiative to promote school and family partnerships, the project delineated the following new assumptions:

- Families and school staff together decide meaningful ways for parents to be involved: as teachers, supporters, advocates, decision makers, ambassadors, and monitors.
- All parents can be resources for their children's schools. Schools must recognize and cultivate the knowledge and strength of each family.

- Diversity is a strength. School culture must reflect the diversity of the school community.
- Decisions are made collaboratively. Everyone has knowledge and has children's best interests at heart.
- Families, schools, and communities hold each other accountable. (Teaching for Change, n.d.)

Re-visiting Decision Making

Most school districts have clear guidelines regarding who is in charge of decision making. Boards of education are usually in charge of creating policies, monitoring budget expenditures, and approving plans and initiatives that administrators are in charge of developing and executing. The Cabinet, which consists of district-level administrators, typically makes decisions regarding day-to-day district operations, instruction, and direction. Ideally, all of the important decisions are made with input from families and the community at large, which school leaders obtain and consider.

Community and Parental Surveys and Feedback

To incorporate voices of parents and community members in decision making, school leaders often employ surveys that help them gauge their community's reaction or attitude toward a particular initiative. On the other hand, one frequent frustration that parents and community members have after investing time and effort in gathering and compiling substantial feedback is that this feedback doesn't matter. Why might this be the case?

One reason is that a request for feedback comes after all of the major decisions and planning have taken place, leaving families and communities with no say other than whether they support or don't support what is being proposed by school administrators. Such a black-and-white approach doesn't consider other possibilities or modifications to the proposal. Another reason is that administrators seem to ignore the input that contradicts their own beliefs or, worse, become defensive if faced with an alternative point of view. For surveys to work, school leaders have to be honest and very clear about the purpose, goals, use, and intentions of a survey.

- Purpose: Is it an effort to understand the community and to listen to other voices or is it a checkmark that all stakeholders were consulted?
- Goal: Is it an effort to establish what works best, even if it means a change in directions, or is it an effort to secure approval?
- Use: Will results be used to inform decision making or will they be skimmed for evidence in support of the preferred direction?

- Intentions: Will results be shared with the public regardless of what they are or will this depend on the results? How will the community be notified what actions are taken as a result of this survey?

It is important to note that school leaders are most likely not intentionally ignoring some feedback, but rather making decisions according to their own prior knowledge and beliefs. The human brain interprets information subjectively, based on an individual's convictions, and it reacts with an immediate rejection as not viable to anything that doesn't fit the profile.

> We form our beliefs for a variety of subjective, personal, emotional, and psychological reasons in the context of environments created by family, friends, colleagues, culture, and society at large; after forming our beliefs we then defend, justify, and rationalize them with a host of intellectual reasons, cogent arguments, and rational explanations. Beliefs come first, explanations for beliefs follow. (Shermer, 2012, p. 5)

This holds true for any human being, regardless of whether it is a parent, an educator, or an administrator. Therefore, to allow feedback to be objectively considered in decision making, a system that will afford this objectivity should be developed and put in place. The system must have clear guidelines and protocols for compiling, analyzing, reporting, and applying feedback to specific decisions:

- Establish and write down a goal: What specifically is this feedback going to determine?
- Put in place a process of how feedback is going to be recorded and results are going to be assembled.
- Create clear criteria for feedback interpretation.
- Assign a person who will be in charge of compiling feedback into a report.
- Select a reviewer (a third party who can look at the results and provide a recommendation).
- Decide on how the results of this report and consequent decisions will be shared with the community.
- Beta test the survey with a small sample of the total intended audience to ascertain clarity and completeness.

Re-designing Decision-Making Bodies

One area that is receiving a lot of attention now in educational organizations is how to restructure decision-making processes, committees, and groups to include voices of major stakeholders, especially families. Many school districts have committees or teams comprising administrators, teachers, board members, community members, and parents that meet several times a year to discuss initiatives considered by district or school administrators.

A potential issue with these committees is, again, a lack of objectivity. Schools control whom they wish to invite on a team, frequently omitting people whose perspectives might not align with those of school leaders. In addition, stakeholders are few in numbers. Two to three parents, for example, who attend meetings are likely to express their own points of view that might or might not be shared by most district parents. There are a lot of limitations to such input, including parents' socioeconomic and individual bias, experiences with schools attended by their children, and their children's academic strengths and weaknesses. Although schools do gain some parental presence in these committees, they never hear the voice of district parents.

Another potential issue is that most committees are advisory in nature. As valuable as it may be, sharing opinions and suggesting ideas is not the same thing as making a decision on whether an initiative should be implemented and, even less so, on how exactly it should be implemented. Discussions often don't receive any further follow-up from school leaders, and whether leaders act on the committee's advice or reject it is also often unknown.

Boards of Education, of course, should represent the community in all matters, but board members, too, are governed by the rules and regulations of their organization. Many of them don't have children in the school systems they serve, which removes them from the firsthand consequences of their decisions.

To include voices of all school community's stakeholders in decisions that require major shifts in assessments, curriculum, or educational practices in general, it is necessary to restructure the district governing body. People support what they create. Representatives of prevalent school- or district-affiliated organizations (e.g., PTAs/PTOs, education associations, education foundations) should be made part of a governing organ, such as the Extended Cabinet, for example. Each representative should be held accountable for working with members of his or her organization to determine the position of the majority. In this case, the voice of a representative will be backed up by hundreds or even thousands of stakeholders.

DEVELOPING INTERNAL PARTNERSHIPS

Most schools and school districts have a number of affiliated organizations that can become their valuable partners in education. Although the majority of these organizations operate at a school level, there are some that function at a district level as well.

School leaders will want to include well-established organizations like the PTA to engage parents affiliated with education advocacy groups, parent-leadership programs, and disability groups. The key is finding organizations or groups that help parents develop the skills to communicate their concerns and interests while also providing the necessary support to keep their constituents well informed. (Blank & McGuire, 2016, p. 28)

Typically, PTAs and PTOs have the largest membership among all of these organizations. Though, in essence, school-based PTOs and PTAs are largely serving the same purpose, PTAs belong to a much larger network, including their state and national PTAs. Districts that have schools with PTA units are likely to also have a district-level parental organization—a PTA Council—that coordinates the work of individual school PTAs. PTA councils could become powerful partners of school districts in developing comprehensive learning environments for students.

District-Level Parental Associations

For more than a hundred years, the National Parent Teacher Association (NPTA), the largest child advocacy association in the United States (currently consisting of more than four million members), has been trying to elevate the work of its individual units by providing them with multiple resources and encouraging them to influence the decisions that affect students' education at their schools, districts, and states. The organization that is dedicated to children's educational success, health, and well-being through strong family and community engagement is known as one of the strongest and most powerful advocates for excellent education for each child.

This makes PTA councils, whose scope of work usually targets district-level initiatives, a natural ally of district administrators, who are interested in developing partnerships with parents and the community. PTA councils or similar district-level organizations that are governed by parents or members of the community represent voices of their members in working for quality education. Though not perfect, their perspectives could serve as a barometer of community feelings, giving feedback to administrators in a more accurate, objective way.

Collaboration could include a variety of joint initiatives, such as parent education and decision making, as described earlier, as well as creating awareness and advocacy to mobilize community to action. If superintendents understand the value of these organizations and seek their input in decisions and processes affecting learning in their districts, they will likely gain rich internal resources that otherwise must be obtained from external consultants.

Because PTA councils and other district-level organizations have a network of school-level organizations that can solicit help and feedback from families throughout the district, working with councils can greatly facilitate processes of sharing information, receiving feedback, and joint decision making with parents. To enable a council–administration alliance around learning and to get the most benefits from this frequently untapped resource, district administrators might consider the following:

- Becoming members of one of their local units represented by a council (or a similar district-level organization) and attending this organization's meetings to understand its work and dynamics
- Scheduling and holding regular meetings with the councils' leaders to share ideas and plans for the district and to discuss initiatives requiring collaboration
- Asking councils to design a plan for creating awareness or engagement strategies that involve families in learning; present this plan to cabinets for further discussions
- Actively soliciting help and advice on how to improve student learning environments by helping families understand instruction, standards, assessments, and performance data
- Seeking advice on revisions and content changes for major district communications intended for families and communities, especially when a new learning/assessment initiative is being considered
- Inviting councils' representatives to share their ideas and concerns regarding parental engagement and learning-related matters with district principals and staff during principal and all staff meetings
- Including councils' representatives into district governance, such as the Extended Cabinet
- Jointly developing concrete proposals for student learning improvement and recommending them to local school boards

Administrators' relationships with parental organizations have to be based on respect, trust, effective communication, and the shared purpose of supporting student success. Such partnerships can have the real power to positively shift parent–teacher relationships and to shape a macro learning environment of the community. Not all school districts, even those with local PTA units, have a PTA council or district-level parental organizations, but if they do, these organizations shouldn't be ignored.

Parent Advisory Boards

District leaders can also partner with individual schools' parental organizations to ensure coherency of learning environments and to build collaboration in the educational process. The difference here, as compared with working with a district-level parental organization, is that it usually becomes the responsibility of district administrators to create an opportunity for parent leaders to assemble regularly and to participate in the work of the district. In many school districts, this opportunity exists in the form of Parent Advisory Boards or Teams.

Parent Advisory Boards are groups usually comprising each school's PTA/PTO leaders or representatives, who meet monthly with superintendents and other district administrators. These boards or teams, however, do not automatically endow partnerships. Although district leaders might see the purpose of these boards in involving parents in decision making, oftent, they utilize these meetings to "hand down" the decisions made by administrators or to inform parents about budget situations, legislative actions, and other district needs.

Following old assumptions and models, administrators frequently do the talking and parents do the listening and note taking. Administrators also compile agenda for the meetings and indicate times for parents to share their school news (usually, at the end of meetings). When district leaders do ask for parental input into initiatives considered by the district, these requests are only rarely supported by structures for collecting this feedback and for reporting back on the actions, taken as a result of this feedback.

It is not enough to just inform parent leaders and to randomly collect concerns and suggestions for improvement. To be effective, a Parent Advisory Board has to have established purpose and expectations of all its members. In Bellingham Public Schools, Washington, for example, members of the Parent Advisory Board work together to:

- Identify common needs and goals among the parents of students enrolled at Bellingham Public Schools and facilitate strategies to increase the efficiency and effectiveness of their respective school's parent organizations
- Provide the superintendent with feedback and insight from the parent's perspective on school process, policies, and initiatives to ensure that the needs of parents and their families are included as decisions are made in the district
- Bring to the superintendent's attention existing and emerging issues expressed by parents at the school they represent
- Serve as an advisory, not a decision making, body that makes recommendations, encourages brainstorming, and provides opportunities for parent involvement on committees and task forces
- Facilitate communication between and among the parents and parent organizations from different district schools and serve as a forum for sharing

innovations and best practices from around the district. (Bellingham Public Schools, n.d.)

In addition, all of the members of a Parent Advisory Board should be accountable for taking requests and information to their schools, soliciting perspectives, and delivering feedback at a consecutive meeting. Superintendents should be accountable for following up on parental concerns, taking action as needed, and updating parents on these actions.

School-Level Parental Organizations

Unlike district-level parental organizations, individual school units are usually not very actively involved in district-wide initiatives, focusing their efforts on the needs of their schools. At a school level, partnerships may imply collaboration between the principal and the PTA/PTO board on initiatives regarding parental engagement in student learning, as well as inclusion of some representatives of the board into collaborative learning, information sharing, and collective planning.

In the book *Beyond the Bake Sale* (2007), Anne Henderson and her colleagues outlined important aspects of school–family partnerships centered on learning, noticing frequent tension areas in parent–teacher–staff relationships, such as student learning feedback, conflict resolution, and sharing power. They delineated, among many others, the following indicators of partnerships in schools:

- There is a clear, open process for resolving problems.
- Teachers contact families each month to discuss student progress.
- Parents and teachers research issues such as prejudice and tracking.
- Parent groups are focused on improving student achievement.
- Families are involved in all major decisions.
- Parents can use the school's phone, copier, fax, and computers. (Henderson et al, 2007, pp. 151–182).

School administrators don't have to work alone on engaging parental community in their schools. Parent leaders can provide valuable insights and assist with many aspects of partnership development. Here are some initiatives that principals might consider for their schools as ways to nurture partnerships with their parental organizations:

- Initiate a discussion, outside of a regular board meeting, with PTA/PTO leaders about the school's teacher–parent interactions and parental perception of the school culture in respect to partnerships.

- Solicit PTA/PTO's written feedback on areas of concern and in need of improvement.
- Ask school parent leaders to survey parents and to gather their suggestions on how to improve teacher–parent interactions around student learning, communications, and two-way feedback.
- Establish a school partnership committee, consisting of PTA/PTO representatives, teachers, staff members, and a principal, to jointly develop new understandings and processes and to communicate them to all stakeholders.
- Enlist PTA/PTO's help to decide which learning opportunities to offer to parents.
- Ask parent leaders to join staff trainings and meetings to gain better insight into new methodologies and learning philosophies.
- Discuss with parent leaders new initiatives, such as adoption of a social–emotional or behavioral intervention program, to gain their perspectives on which programs resonate the most with families.
- Provide joint learning opportunities to parent leaders and staff (e.g., if teachers are reading a book on new methodology or a learning approach, a copy of this book could be offered to the parental organization).
- Communicate how PTA/PTO's feedback is applied to decision making.
- Keep parent leaders informed by including them in staff e-mail communications (as appropriate).

Parent leaders should be encouraged to share their ideas regarding student learning and general parental concerns with a principal and school staff. Attending staff meetings and having face-to-face discussions with educators in a non-confrontational manner could be very effective in building trust and in opening a productive dialogue about student learning.

ENTERING EXTERNAL COLLABORATIONS

Many school districts nowadays are combining their resources together with other learning institutions and community organizations to provide students with improved educational opportunities, different career pathways, and easier transitions to colleges. As a result of these partnerships, students are often instructed by the teaching staff of other educational entities (and possibly physically spend some time there as well) and receive credit toward their graduation requirements at their own district. This involves numerous considerations of logistics, staff qualification, and financing, so partnerships of this kind usually require a lot of planning. However, when thoroughly implemented, these collaborations significantly expand and enhance students' learning environments.

Partnerships with Other Learning Organizations

Colleges

Dual enrollment partnerships are established between school districts and local colleges to enable high school students to enroll into college courses while they are still enrolled in their high school. Colleges are expensive; when students can take their general education college courses while still in high school, it benefits them not only academically but also financially. Dual enrollment programs can vary widely and cater to the needs of particular schools and districts. In some programs, dual enrollment classes take place in high school during the school day. Other programs require students to attend regular classes on the college campus. It is up to both partners to decide the terms of a dual enrollment.

Articulation agreements with local colleges is another way to help students earn college credits in their high school Career and Technical Education courses. An agreement is usually entered into by the college instructors and high school teachers if they feel that the skills and competencies acquired by students in both institutions are very compatible and students would like to continue their education in a related program of study. Through articulation agreements, colleges give college credit for some courses taken in high school. High school instructors are accountable for delivering quality instruction and for verifying that students have achieved specific levels of competency.

Intermediate School Districts and Technical Campuses

Career and Technical Education campuses become available to school districts through collaboration with their Intermediate School Districts (ISD) or community colleges. Learning at a technical campus is a valuable extension of students' high school learning that allows them to fulfill their graduation requirements while also working toward earning college credits and certifications. The key strength of Career and Technical education is in helping students explore various career directions and obtain skills that allow them to enter directly into well-paying, skilled jobs. Since students will be spending a part of their school day at a technical campus, transportation is always something to consider.

Early College is an option that often results from partnerships between intermediate school districts and colleges. Usually, 11th- and 12th-grade students take college courses along with coursework at their home high school and, potentially, technical campus. The difference between an early college and some other opportunities, such as a dual enrollment, for example, is that students have to commit to attending a particular college full-time during an added 13th year. This extends their opportunities to earn both their associate's degree and high school diploma without having to pay for college tuition or books. Individual school districts can work with their ISDs to offer this possibility to students.

Virtual Learning Providers

The majority of the colleges nowadays offer online classes that create viable options for many high school students. In addition, virtual learning partnerships could be developed with learning organizations that offer interactive learning platforms and courses. In these cases, students will have multiple opportunities to take classes online to accommodate their needs and to receive credit toward their graduation requirements.

Shared Services

Shared Services is an agreement between two learning organizations to set up and operate shared services. The key here is the idea of sharing resources between organizations. In 2010, the state of Michigan created a program that gave public schools an opportunity to provide services to the private schools in the non-core and elective areas, such as art, computers, foreign languages, music, physical education, and other non-core curricular activities.

Such agreements enable public school districts to provide their educators to the private schools and to receive proportional funding from the state for the number of private school students in these classes. Public schools can also hire highly qualified private schools' teachers to offer instruction to public school students. This creates more course options for all students and expands their learning environments. Since sharing services does involve a lot of financial configurations and the shared accountability for learning outcomes, these partnerships require detailed agreements.

Partnerships with Community Groups, Agencies, and Organizations

It is very difficult, if not impossible, for schools to engage entire communities on their own. Therefore, entering a variety of partnerships and coalitions with community groups and various organizations could be very beneficial to schools in a sense that they can build on the pre-existing relationships of these organizations. In addition, organizations usually have resources that help foster a powerful macro learning environment.

Thus, schools and districts should become simultaneously engaged in a multitude of collaborative partnerships of various orientations, which can assist them in meeting the needs of all learners. Each community-based coalition has to begin with a clear understanding of its purpose, goals, and deliverables; this largely determines whether the partnership succeeds.

Learning-oriented partnerships are collaborations with community organizations that result in additional learning opportunities and instructional services that count toward students' graduation requirements or credit in a particular subject. Businesses and organizations, in these cases, act as learning providers. Usually, these partnerships are focused on offering students advanced learning opportunities that schools cannot provide on their own.

- Subject-specific partnerships create opportunities for students, who demonstrate substantial accomplishments in a non-core subject, to continue instruction in an advanced setting. If a student is an accomplished artist, musician, or gymnast, for example, this student may have an option to leave school early and to attend voice/instrument/art lessons or gymnastics practice at a local conservatory, an art school, or a gymnastics academy. The lessons are attended in lieu of art, band (choir), or physical education courses regularly taken at schools or as an elective course.
- Apprentice partnerships result in curriculum-related instruction and on-the-job training that are simultaneously provided by businesses or community organizations where learning takes place. These workshops can be attended by students who are interested in acquiring specific trade skills as an alternative to taking a regular Career and Technical Education class at school.
- Internships agreements between schools and local organizations enable students to receive training in a specific profession and to earn money while doing it. Usually, internships are provided in summer months and are counted toward graduation requirements.

Service-oriented partnerships between schools and community organizations offer students opportunities to develop important dispositions, skills, and character traits while helping others.

- Academic Service Learning—a classroom-based program that involves students in community service as a means of understanding course concepts—requires partnerships with external organizations, where this service can be delivered. This approach to learning provides many important benefits to students, brings awareness to community issues, and provides short- and long-term solutions to community needs. Partnerships with Habitat for Humanity, Red Cross, Girl Scouts of America, or any charity organization can help create opportunities for such learning.
- Volunteering, similarly to Academic Service Learning, stems from partnerships with external organizations and helps students develop

dispositions of care and empathy by helping their community. Local animal shelters can always use volunteers to clean cages, answer phones, or help out with some tasks around the shelter, for example. If students can get involved in giving back to their community in a meaningful way, the benefits are far-reaching.

Enrichment-oriented partnerships are focused on providing students with additional opportunities for learning. Schools can partner with individual community organizations, Parks and Recreation services, libraries, art museums, music halls, programs, or businesses.

- After-School Clubs/Activities: Schools can collaborate with organizations and businesses to offer students activities at schools' locations free of charge or at a reduced rate. Since attending these activities doesn't require transportation, many students, who otherwise stay at a latchkey program, may be able to enjoy a game of soccer, learning to play chess, or listening to a story read by a local librarian.
- Tutoring: On-site tutoring opportunities provided by local tutoring services indicate another good way to collaborate with the community and to ensure that there is coherency between classroom instruction and tutoring.
- On-site subject-focused camps during school breaks, for example, a writing camp, poetry camp, math camp, science camp, or anything else that gives a student in-depth exploration of a subject, could be considered.
- School gardens: Schools can partner with a local garden club and with nurseries to create and maintain a garden at their school locations. Students can participate in gardening and develop an understanding of curriculum-related concepts by observing processes that take place in nature.
- Art and Music education: Partnerships with museums, art galleries, orchestra halls, and conservatories provide students and their families with educational experiences at their locations.

Student care-oriented partnerships are usually formed between schools and community organizations to ensure that the basic needs of their students are met. The benefits of these partnerships can drastically improve learning conditions for many students. These are some things that community partners could provide for students if schools are willing to act as coordinators:

- After-school care (local religious institutions or seniors)
- Transportation (any organization in possession of vehicles)
- Free meals (restaurants and grocery stores)
- Free emergency medical and dental care (a network of local physicians and dentists)

- School supplies (local office supplies stores)
- Mentoring (local organizations)

Prevention-oriented partnerships are aimed at creating awareness and generating community activism to address substance-related or similar problems. These partnerships are formed between schools and organizations working specifically on issues in need of prevention. Presence of drugs, underage drinking, and violence are some of the issues requiring prevention.

Inviting family and community collaboration around learning should become a priority at schools as one of the most effective strategies to create a powerful learning environment for every child. Although there are many individual circumstances and variations within school districts, all partnerships are based on the same principles of trust, sharing, and joint decision making.

School leaders should not be asking their families and communities to merely support their own projects and ideas; they should involve their partners into a project from its brainstorming stage and throughout its completion. All of the parties in a partnership must share ownership and be accountable for doing their part. The barriers have to be lifted to allow the full use of human capital, regardless of who is who in the district. Collective work for the benefit of students takes priority over paperwork, political considerations, and personal attitudes of the partners.

The success does require an investment of time, effort, and resources. However, it is necessary to realize that investing into a culture of partnerships wherein families, communities, and schools share responsibility for student learning leads to enormous positive outcomes in many areas, the most important of which is student learning.

REFLECT ON THIS

1. Does my district or school mission include parents and the community? If not, how can I make this happen?
2. Do my district's policies allow me to include parents and the community into decision making? How can these policies be adjusted?
3. Have I established clear expectations for my administrators and teachers regarding partnering with families? For what exactly are they held accountable in their work with families?
4. Do I include parents in district/school decision making? Are parents serving on improvement planning teams or other committees that are accountable for sharing information and delivering a collective parental voice (not just their personal opinion)?

5. Do I have a line item in my budget for family engagement? Who is responsible for proactively working on family engagement?
6. Do I attend a district-level (school-level) parental organization's meeting, at least occasionally?
7. Do I include parent leaders in staff professional development, at least occasionally?
8. Do I invite parent leaders to attend my Cabinet and staff meetings? How can I make this happen?
9. During the previous meeting with representatives of my district or school parental organizations, who did most of the talking and sharing? How did I capture parental input? What action items did parents take with them from it? What could have been done differently?
10. If I would like to form one partnership with parents or a community organization today, what is the first step to doing this?

Chapter 6 Snapshot: SUPPORTING COLLABORATION

FOCUS AREA	COMMON PRACTICE	WHAT TO CONSIDER
Institutionalization and Policies	Policies focused on purposes, activities, and financial accountability of affiliated organizations	Mission statement includes families and communities as full-rights partners in education. Strategic Plan includes steps for building capacity for partnerships with various stakeholders. New policies and procedures remove barriers, allow schools to form partnerships around student learning, and provide the structure for involving families and communities in decision making. Professional development of staff on building and sustaining family–community partnerships
Decision Making	Families and communities are asked to support or to provide feedback on schools' decisions	Families and communities make decisions together with schools; representatives, selected by parental and community organizations, are included into schools' decision-making bodies.

FOCUS AREA	COMMON PRACTICE	WHAT TO CONSIDER
Internal Partnerships	Parent Advisory Boards run by school administrators	District-level parental organizations—e.g., PTA councils, Special Education, and Gifted and Talented organizations School-level parental organizations Other district-affiliated organizations that are not governed by schools
External Partnerships	Other learning institutions Intermediate school districts Technical campuses Community colleges Universities	Partnerships with community groups, agencies, and organizations: Learning-oriented partnerships Service-oriented partnerships Enrichment-oriented partnerships Student care-oriented partnerships Prevention-oriented partnerships

Chapter Seven

Partners in Special Needs and Circumstances

We have no special needs children. Just children…with special needs.

—Uwe Maurer

One rather obvious fact that determines student learning is only slowly gaining some response in education: Every learner is human. Learning doesn't happen separately from students' lives; rather, it is a direct result of processes and experiences affecting them as human beings. How a student learns depends on types of his or her prevalent intelligences (Gardner, 1995), processing speed, as well as socioeconomic, cultural, and biological factors.

There are many learners in American schools who have special needs. Some of these needs stem from their home and community environments; some are determined by how their brains process information and react to their surroundings. Either way, if these needs are not met, students are unlikely to grow as leaners and to achieve their full potential. As important as school–family–community partnerships are for any child's learning, for success of these students, they become vital.

PARTNERS IN ADVERSITY

When humans experience hunger and other deficits associated with poverty, it is not learning that occupies their minds. Daily survival becomes the main goal, which is often accompanied by chronic stress and disengagement from school. Many high school–age students drop out of schools to help their families, seeing this as a number one priority.

There are parents who work long hours or whose own school experiences left them with no trust in educational institutions. There are families who speak other languages or have different cultural beliefs about roles of schools and parents. Students in many circumstances have little support at home, whereas their learning environments might be drastically different from the ones that educators are striving to create at schools, which often substantially impedes their performance.

A report from the Organization for Economic Co-Operation and Development (OECD, 2016), which analyzes low-performing students across the globe, offers very compelling statistics:

> On average across OECD countries, a student of average socio-economic status who is a boy living in a two-parent family, has no immigrant background, speaks the same language at home as in school, lives in a city, attended more than one year of pre-primary education, did not repeat a grade and attends a general curricular track (or school) has a 10% probability of low performance in mathematics, while a student with the same socio-economic status but who is a girl living in a single-parent family, has an immigrant background, speaks a different language at home than at school, lives in a rural area, did not attend pre-primary school, repeated a grade and attends a vocational track has a 76% probability of low performance. (p. 62)

The report makes it clear that it is a lack of opportunities that leads to low performance. Thus, as OECD's Director for Education and Skills, Andreas Schleicher (2016), suggests in his Foreword, education policy and practice can help students gain more opportunities. Schleicher believes that education practices have to encompass multiple dimensions, including creating supporting learning environments and involving parents and communities:

- Creating demanding and supportive learning environments
- Involving parents and local communities
- Inspiring students to make the most of available education opportunities
- Identifying low performers and providing targeted support for students, schools, and families
- Offering special programs for immigrant, minority-language, and rural students
- Tackling gender stereotypes
- Reducing inequalities in access to early education and limiting the use of student sorting. (p. 3)

Creating Awareness

In its concept, the process of creating awareness when working with marginalized families is not very different from what was described in chapter 5 of this book. Awareness is essential in providing the understanding of what children are learning and what they are expected to accomplish as learners. However, while creating a communication system in a school district with large numbers of low-income families or immigrant communities, it is necessary to consider which additional information needs to be included and how to reach families based on their customs, ability to understand English, level of education, and at-home technology.

Content-wise, schools need to create awareness about factors that affect student learning. One important challenge in educating children in poor neighborhoods and some immigrant communities is that students frequently miss school. There might be many reasons for this to happen—from transportation issues to parents' need to pull a child from school to help with interpreting when they visit banks, immigration offices, or employment agencies. Some cultures believe that teens have to work or girls don't need education. It is important, therefore, to reinforce an understanding that school attendance is important.

In 2012, 22 states treated "failure to educate" as child neglect. In New York, where around 40% of high school students missed 20 or more days of school each year, parents of students with a lot of absences were reported to the child protective system (Marcus, 2012, July/August, p. 1). This, of course, can lead to removing a child to foster care. Thus, part of learning-related communication should be focused on making parents aware of state laws and regulations regarding their responsibility to ensure that their child receives an education and on helping them better understand how showing up for school affects their children's learning.

Another important area of communication tends to be information on the resources that are available to parents to obtain health care so that their child is able to attend school.

> Children in poverty are as much as 16 times more likely than middle-class and affluent children to have asthma, which is blamed for 12.8 million missed school days annually. They're twice as likely to have unmet dental needs, according to the U.S. Surgeon General's office. The Baltimore Student Attendance Campaign reports that another two million school days nationwide are lost each year to dental-related illnesses. And when they are in class, at least 25 percent of urban students may not be able to see the blackboard. That's how many are estimated to have unaddressed vision problems. (Marcus, 2012, July/August, p.1)

Schools need to widely and frequently share information on how schools work to meet needs of students, what opportunities are available to them, and how this will benefit them and their families in the future. Making parents aware of free health clinics or government provisions that might be of an advantage to them can lead to improved attendance and increased learning.

Schools and districts that strive to provide such information to their families often find it difficult, however, to reach those who need this information the most. Rural and very low-income parents without an easy access to Internet, computers, or smart phones might not be able to communicate electronically. In such cases, teacher–parent or school–parent communication cannot rely on e-mails, websites, Facebook pages, and Twitter accounts. Printed weekly classroom communications and monthly district and school newsletters mailed directly to homes may be a necessity.

Finally, it is important to communicate in a manner that is easy to understand. Educational jargon and advanced vocabulary, long complex sentences, or lengthily legal explanations create a barrier to understanding. In predominantly non-English-speaking communities, district communication could become more effective if it accommodated the language of the community and contained a translated version in addition to the English original.

Seeking Engagement

Low-income and non-English-speaking families may be intimidated by the school system. To engage these families in student learning could require additional steps, especially initially. If parents are apprehensive about coming into school, teachers can alleviate this anxiety by meeting them where they are the most comfortable and where they don't feel threatened—their homes. Spending one-on-one time with students' families seems to be a very successful strategy for involving hard-to-reach parents in schools and student learning. Many districts now are starting the year off with teacher visits to students' homes, which serves as an invitation to parents to become partners in their children's education.

Time with Families

Home visits can welcome parents into the education process. There are many benefits that come with them. Visiting a student's house places a teacher inside a child's home learning environment, provides an insight into family circumstances, allows them to learn from parents, and gives an opportunity to establish trust. A home visit, however, doesn't automatically mean that parents will become engaged or teachers will leave with a good grasp on a child's personality or situation. What an educator does and says while at a student's home can either bring families in or leave them at a distance.

Shane Safiris, a leader, an educational coach, and the founder of June Jordan School for Equity for low-income students in San Francisco, sees listening as the most powerful tool to promote family engagement: It helps build relational capital with some of the most marginalized families. During her home visits, she took the time to sit down with parents as a listener—to be fully present, alert, with no tables or desk separating her from families—and to ask them for their hopes and dreams for their child, expectations for their academic performance and behavior, as well as expectations of educators.

Safiris recommends the following while visiting families:

- Be mindful of power, status, and non-verbal communication.
- Ask families for feedback.
- Listen more than you talk.
- Ask meaningful questions.
- Use active listening techniques by paraphrasing what you've heard and ensure that little is lost in interpretation. (as cited in Ferlazzio, 2016, January 23)

Home visits don't have to be linked to a one-time-only occurrence before a school year begins. Subsequent visits can be very helpful in providing parents with some coaching on how to help their child and in offering suggestions on developing certain skills at home. Subsequent visits can also uncover why students experience problems and what teachers and parents can do together to eliminate these problems.

Learning Systems

Educating parents and caregivers in the districts with many adversity factors is directly connected to increased family engagement and student learning. Ronald Ferguson's (2002) study of more than 30,000 racially diverse students in urban areas suggested that in "response to differences in family background advantages, schools could supply more educational resources and learning experiences outside the home, by providing access to books and computers and extra curricular opportunities for intellectual enrichment" (p. 21).

To accomplish this, schools have to commit resources to developing family-friendly systems. Everything—from open classrooms and community visits to parental workshops and parent academies—will contribute to knowledge, understanding, and, consequently, engagement. However, to make a radical difference in low-income communities, there is often a need for an extensive and comprehensive model: a systemic community-wide learning program for parents and structures that support it.

A Parent University can become such a learning system that helps bridge information gaps by offering families a rounded understanding of learning, parenting, children's emotional and mental well-being, as well as what they can do to create healthy learning environments at home. Parent Universities can offer a variety of learning opportunities in response to the needs of the community.

For example, in immigrant communities, a Parent University can include English as second-language classes; whereas in rural communities, an additional emphasis might be on computer literacy. School- or district-based family centers, where families access technology, find books recommended by teachers, or take adult education classes, are also very impactful in engaging parents in learning. These centers can also become learning locations for a Parent University.

When Howard Lewis Parent Center in Buffalo Public Schools in New York opened in 1989, it was one of the first in the country. By 2002, the center offered services and activities for the district's 44,000 students and their families. It provided two computer labs with more than 50 computers and 60 laptops for families to take home to work together at home with their children. Among the 22 staff members working at the center, there were seven specialists in adult and early childhood education, a computer skills teacher, and district teachers who served as mathematics, reading, and language specialists.

There were many learning activities for parents and children to do together with the help of college tutors. Transportation to the center, which was open year-round, was provided for parents by the district. Each school building in the district was also requested to create a parent area for families to meet or complete volunteer projects (*Educating Our Children Together*, n.d., p. 34). Realistically, of course, any large-scale endeavor requires funding and not always is it possible to create an entire comprehensive model at once. Whatever funds and efforts schools can put into parental engagement is a start.

Supporting Collaboration

Since 1965, Title I—the federal program that was created to supply funding to improve the academic achievement of disadvantaged students—has been allocating federal funds to schools with high numbers or high percentages of children from low-income families, based on census poverty estimates and the cost of education in each state. U.S. Department of Education's most recent data on participation in the program show that

> In 2009-10 more than 56,000 public schools across the country used Title I funds to provide additional academic support and learning opportunities to help low-achieving children master challenging curricula and meet state standards in core academic subjects. For example, funds support extra instruction in reading and mathematics, as well as special preschool, after-school, and summer programs to extend and reinforce the regular school curriculum. That same year Title I served more than 21 million children. Of these students, approximately 59 percent were in kindergarten through fifth grade, 21 percent in grades 6-8,

17 percent in grades 9-12, 3 percent in preschool, and less than one percent ungraded. (U.S. Department of Education, n.d.)

It is getting progressively clear that investing in fragmented measures that are focused on the content or methodology, without taking care of students' essential needs outside of school, is not going to solve problems in the long term for many students. To some degree, this is similar to replacing windows and doors in a house, whose foundation can give up at any moment. In attempting to fix this foundation, Columbia University Teacher College launched the Campaign for Educational Equity (CEE) that proposes the Comprehensive Educational Opportunity Project, a full-service system of resources and support for students in poverty.

> These resources include traditional educational resources like high-quality teaching, a rich and rigorous curriculum, adequate facilities, and sufficient, up-to-date learning materials. In addition, they must include supplemental re-sources needed to overcome the impediments to educational achievement imposed by the conditions of poverty. Extensive research in this area has emphasized four fundamental areas of requisite preventive and supportive services: (1) early childhood education beginning from birth; (2) routine and preventive physical and mental health care; (3) after-school, summer school, and other expanded learning time programs; and (4) family engagement and support. (Rebell, 2012, p. 53)

Having a full-service school or district that offers health and dental care, along with meeting other needs of students, is a goal that needs to be considered by any K–12 educational institution that has Title 1 students. Title 1 funds are frequently spent on additional learning opportunities for students, so partnerships with communities, organizations, businesses, and other educational establishments often become viable avenues to offer more support to students and their families.

Terry Thomas, an art teacher at Seaton Elementary School in Washington, DC, is the liaison for several partnerships at her school: the Kennedy Center, the Embassy Adoption Program through the Washington Performing Arts Society, the Architecture in the Schools, the Arts for Every Student through the DC Arts Collaborative, and the Children are Citizens program. In addition, she participates in the school's family engagement program. According to Thomas, her Title I students and families greatly benefit from these partnership programs:

> Were it not for my school's involvement with these ongoing partnerships, our students and their families would not have access to the many cultural and academic experiences directly offered through these programs. Throughout the

year—on weekends and some evenings—I organize trips for students and their families to cultural events. This is a door opener for many families who may be reluctant to venture or explore outside their immediate surroundings. (personal communication, 2016, May 21)

In Pontiac Schools, Michigan, there is a network of community partners, including members of local professional organizations, businesses, and churches, who, in coordinated collaboration, back the district's schools. Some partners offer tutoring services and enrichment opportunities, whereas others make sure that students' essential needs are met. Partners donate uniforms for schools, provide transportation, supply food, and do whatever is needed to ensure that every child has access to quality education.

If seeking to meet students' needs outside of school through student care-oriented partnerships, districts could try some of the following:

- Reach out to local religious institutions and senior centers to secure free after-school care and transportation from schools to homes
- Collaborate with local grocery stores and local branches of charity organizations, such as Blessings in the Backpack, for example, to supply students and their families with free groceries
- Establish an agreement with restaurants to deliver free meals to families
- Create a network of local physicians and dentists who are willing to donate their time
- Enlist the help of local gardeners to build a garden at each school where students can volunteer, learn, and use what they grow to supplement school lunches
- Collaborate with local counselors to donate time counseling students with emotional issues

Since children from neighborhoods with concentrated poverty face overwhelming odds in their communities, students need to see immediate as well as long-term value in education as the way "out" to a different life. This is also true about their families, who are more likely to ensure student attendance if they see tangible benefits of learning. Therefore, districts should be proactively seeking partnerships that could provide students with paying learning opportunities and lead to professional certifications:

- Technical and Career Education partnerships
- Middle and Early College collaborations
- Articulated Credit agreements
- Dual Enrollments

- Apprentice and mentoring programs to earn money while exploring various career options

Whether there is funding or not, schools, families, and communities have to come together to make sure that there are equity, understanding, and a shared vision for their students'/children's future. Schools have always been respected by communities, often looking to them for help and stability. "In a lot of communities, the schools are the only safety net that's left," believes Pedro Noguera, a professor of education at New York University. "Schools should be central as the point of service delivery" (as quoted in Marcus, 2012, July/August, p. 2).

PARTNERS IN SPECIAL NEEDS

Commonly, *special needs* is a general term for a vast variety of conditions that interfere with learning: from learning disabilities, such as Central Auditory Processing Disorder, Dyscalculia, Dyslexia, Language Processing Disorder, and Non-Verbal Learning Disabilities to Cognitive Impairment and developmental delays. The Individuals with Disabilities Education Act (IDEA) was adopted in 1975 by the federal government to mandate that children with disabilities receive instruction that meets their unique needs.

National Center for Education Statistics (2015) reports that even though the overall percentage of total public school enrollment for children who qualified for special education services slightly decreased between 2004–05 (13.8%) and 2011–12 (12.9%),

> The percentage of children identified as having other health impairments (limited strength, vitality, or alertness due to chronic or acute health problems such as a heart condition, tuberculosis, rheumatic fever, nephritis, asthma, sickle cell anemia, hemophilia, epilepsy, lead poisoning, leukemia, or diabetes) rose from 1.1 to 1.5 percent of total public school enrollment, the percentage with autism rose from 0.4 to 0.9 percent, and the percentage with developmental delay rose from 0.7 to 0.8 percent. (para. 2)

Schools have been experiencing a continuous growth in the number of students with autism, Aspergers syndrome, Attention Deficit Disorder (ADD)/ Attention Deficit Hyperactivity Disorder (ADHD), as well as complex medical needs or physical disabilities. In the previous three years, nationwide, the number of 6- to 21-year-old students with autism rose considerably, making it a 165% increase between the 2005–06 and 2014–15 school years.

"Other health impairments," including ADHD, epilepsy or mobility impairments, and mental-health issues increased by about 51% over that same 10-year span (Samuels, 2016, p. 12). All of these students need assistive technology, the right tools, special instruction, and a lot of support, especially at home. For them to learn and grow, families have to be in sync with schools and schools have to be in sync with families.

Not only those who are qualified for special education services are students with special needs. Profoundly gifted children are also special learners. Gifted children usually differ from their peers in terms of social skills, emotional reactivity, and development. Their social and emotional maturity might be far behind their intellectual abilities or they might exhibit extreme sensitivity. In fact, according to Paula Hillmann (2011, April 2) of the Educational Psychology Department at the University of Wisconsin–Madison, some students may be identified with special education needs, in addition to being accelerated learners in other areas: for example, a dyslexic student who has profound potential in creative writing.

Hillmann claims, "several studies in gifted education have concluded that parents are accurate 80-90% of the time when it comes to the identification of their child's abilities and an understanding of their needs. Therefore, collaborative parental involvement is a vital component of successful education" (para. 14). However, parents and children alike often feel isolated and confused, unsure what their course of action should be. Gail Post (2015, August 1), a psychologist who worked with many parents of gifted children, notes that a lot of parents express regrets over not having spoken up sooner or demanded intensive educational services.

At the same time, the Fordham Institute's national study of teachers revealed that 58% of teachers had received no professional development that focused on teaching academically advanced students in the previous few years (Farkas & Duffe, 2008). Even when teachers do realize that a student is gifted, they may not have resources to help the child. In many cases though, giftedness goes undetected.

Creating Awareness

Diagnosis

When working on building partnerships with parents of students with special needs, the Creating Awareness stage might very well start with a diagnosis. Physical and some other pronounced disabilities or profound giftedness are typically detected early in a child's life, whereas many learning disabilities and moderate giftedness often get noticed and diagnosed when children enter an elementary school. Since either difficulties or noticeable mastery well beyond a child's age in reading, writing, and/or math become recognizable during the elementary years, symptoms of these special needs frequently emerge during that time.

Often, it is up to a teacher to take the initial step of letting parents know that a child might need to be evaluated. It is especially important, because "many individuals with learning disabilities may never receive an evaluation and go through life, never knowing why they have difficulties with academics and why they may be having problems in their jobs or in relationships with family and friends" (Learning Disabilities Association of America, n.d.).

Profoundly gifted children also frequently display their abilities in ways that are not recognized in mainstream environments, and their distinguishing characteristics are easily misunderstood. These learners need help in finding supportive environments at both home and school. Thus, teachers can make a difference in children's and families' lives by requesting diagnostics and making parents aware of the condition.

Diagnosis-Specific Information and Resources

When there is a specific diagnosis, it is necessary to continuously communicate with families regarding the special needs of their child, in general, and his or her learning needs, in particular. New research findings and developments are frequently being introduced in professional publications and blogs. Supplying links to such materials is very important to keep families informed. This can be especially far-reaching for children from disadvantaged families, whose parents most likely have very little resources and knowledge of how to support their child. Educators can provide printouts of important articles and help connect parents in similar situations with each other and with appropriate support groups.

Learning-Related Information

Although families of children with special needs may be dealing with different concerns that are specific to their children's diagnosis, all parents must be involved in their child's education by nurturing supportive learning environments, staying aware of what a child is and isn't getting out of school, and advocating for appropriate accommodations. Parents have to be aware of their role and rights, and schools have to communicate this to parents. Teachers or special educators should keep families abreast of learning strategies and effective practices that have proven to advance learning for children with a similar condition.

Most of the parents in special education and gifted and talented programs realize the importance of such information, which makes them more receptive than an average parent to communication coming from schools. System-wise, there is not much difference here from how schools and districts create awareness through various types of media. In addition to regular communication from teachers, some districts design social media pages, dedicated to special education or gifted and talented education, that become a good resource to families and provide them with support and a forum.

Seeking Engagement

For parents of children who qualify for Special Education services, official engagement in their children's learning often starts with participation in their first Individualized Education Plan (IEP)—a process with the purpose of creating an educational plan that enables a child to reach his or her full potential. Ideally, parents collaborate with teachers and special educators as a team to examine a student's present level of academic achievement and functional performance based on his or her disability. They also establish the strengths and specific needs or special factors related to the success of the student. The team creates student-driven goals and objectives for specific content/instructional areas, as well as discusses the need for supplemental aids and service providers in the school setting.

Since parents are uniquely positioned to help their children apply what they learn, they can work on their children's IEP goals outside of the school. Thus, to ensure consistency between school and home learning environments, it is necessary for schools to offer parents opportunities for hands-on learning and techniques that would allow them to understand and support their children's learning. Open classroom lessons and events that permit observations and trials of specific methodologies, techniques, or skills could benefit parents and children to a great extent.

Even greater benefits can be achieved through one-on-one teacher–parent coaching, especially if a teacher takes time to visit students at home, as was done by Marina Garcia, a Special Education teacher from Macomb Intermediate Schools in Michigan. Garcia believes that when parents get one-on-one time with their child's teacher, "they are more willing to take teacher's advice and use the techniques because they know that the teacher is putting in his or her time to see their child succeed" (personal communication, 2016, May 21) (see Textbox 7.1).

For parents of gifted students, schools can create learning opportunities to understand giftedness and how their child might be different from his or her peers. Strategies that help nurture positive learning environments at home for these children always find a lot of interest. Some possibilities include:

- Contacting local teacher colleges to inquire whether there is a gifted education specialist who can run some workshops with parents

---

Textbox 7.1

HANDS-ON COACHING

Marina Garcia, Special Education Teacher,

Lutz School for Work Experience, Macomb Intermediate Schools, MI

In 20 years that I have taught in the Autism Program, I have worked with many families on different issues, but my goal for partnering with parents has always been to help their children lead a better life and be more independent. It is sometimes hard for parents of children with special needs to allow them to do things by themselves. They feel the need to step in and assist their special learners at all times, which makes them depend on parents.

To become more independent, children with Autism Spectrum Disorder (ASD) need additional support and reinforcement to master self-care skills such as feeding themselves, using the toilet, dressing, washing, and taking care of their belongings. Often though, before parents could coach their children, they need to be coached on how to be effective coaches. That is where I felt I could help.

Learning to use the toilet is one important area for children with ASD. As with most self-care skills, teaching toileting works best if the whole routine is broken into smaller steps. I would work on techniques at school first with a child to see what was successful and then arrange a meeting with the parents to go over specific information and strategies for their child, so that they could transfer that knowledge to their home.

I would keep checking with parents on their progress at home to make sure that they are incorporating the same strategies I used at school. As a student's home environment is different from that of a classroom, home visits are often necessary for me to understand what might not go well at home. On a number of occasions, I visited students' houses to help parents right where they needed help most—their homes. Every time I showed them how exactly this could be done at home, it would take a big weight off parents' shoulders. They could see how to be successful without second guessing themselves.

The parents of my students were always very appreciative of the time we, as a team, put together in helping their children be more productive and independent at home. Parents feel better when they know a teacher cares about their child. I believe this is what makes a great teacher–parent team. When a teacher actively shares with parents his or her expertise and gives some quality time to parents regarding issues they are having, the parents have no choice but to be engaged in supporting their student's learning.

- Reaching out to state or national associations for the gifted and talented to provide training
- Offering parents specific tasks to do at home with children
- Putting together a process for a team of parents, teachers, administrators, a student, and an advisor to create a Personal Learning Plan, similar to that of special education students, that will establish some direction for students, parents, and schools alike

- Inviting parents to observe their children while they are in a classroom, followed by sharing and discussing their observations with teachers
- If a school does have a gifted and talented program, opening classrooms for parents to observe learning within this program and affording them opportunities to participate in some activities

Supporting Collaboration

Regardless of what kind of special needs a student has, schools are responsible for making public schools work for each child. The mindset of servant leadership is about supporting children. The first step to making education work for every child is the official recognition and institutionalization of the fact that there are children who require different learning services.

Since 1975, when the *IDEA* made schools legally accountable for educating students with disabilities, most public school districts have created Special Education Services, staffed with various professionals and, often, a director or an assistant superintendent who supervises this department. There are evaluations and processes in place to help identify such learners. Gifted and talented students, however, are frequently not even acknowledged by school districts, whereas some districts altogether deny that giftedness exists.

Collaboration with families at a district level often starts with including parent representatives from Special Education and gifted and talented organizations in a district's decision-making and advisory committees that inform instruction. Creating educational opportunities that can meet diverse needs is a responsibility that has to be shared by teachers, educational specialists, administrators, families, community agencies, and local organizations, often brought together by schools.

When in 2013, Wisconsin Rapids Public School District brought to their Board of Education the *Gifted and Talented Educational Services Plan* (Wisconsin Rapids Public School District, 2013, April 15), the need for it was hard to question. This 52-page document, supported by more than 40 sources, manifested the work of the nine-person Gifted and Talented Educational Services Committee, which in itself was an excellent example of collaboration: Two parents, an elementary teacher, a Gifted and Talented Educational Services (GATES) coordinator, a school psychologist, a building administrator, a secondary teacher, the director of Curriculum and Instruction, and a school counselor brought together their unique perspectives to develop a new program for their district.

Building on the district mission "Working together with home and community, we are dedicated to providing the best education for every student, enabling each to be a thoughtful, responsible contributor to a changing world," GATES officially made education of gifted students a shared responsibility:

Gifted children have unique academic and social and emotional needs. When their needs are not met, there is a loss to the individual, to the school, and to society.

Three of those most basic needs are:

1. An advanced level of challenge and/or pace
2. Socio-emotional fulfillment through interaction with other students of similar abilities
3. Support in dealing with issues such as perfectionism, sensitivity, loneliness, underachievement, and depression

These needs are best met on an ongoing daily basis, within the general education environment, by an appropriately trained school staff with access to adequate resources. This is not the responsibility of one person. All school district staff including administrators, teachers, interventionists, related support staff, GATES Coordinator, psychologists and counselors, as well as parents, must be involved with planning, implementing, supporting, and evaluating the Gifted and Talented Educational Services provided to our students. The students themselves have the responsibility to take advantage of the opportunities and services provided for them. (Wisconsin Rapids Public School District, 2013, April 15, p. 5)

This program utilizes the Wisconsin Response to Intervention three-tiered model and the Wisconsin Comprehensive School Counseling Model as a systemic approach for serving gifted students and sees ongoing staff development, school-wide collaboration, and family involvement as keys to making this model work for students.

Schools can partner with parental organizations, in general, and special education/gifted and talented parent-led councils to bring in professional speakers, such as authors and researchers, to provide additional professional learning opportunities to teachers in these areas. Learning-oriented partnerships to support learning needs of special education and gifted students can be established through collaborations with school-affiliated organizations, community organizations, and other learning institutions.

- Apprentice partnerships formed with local businesses to allow some hands-on learning specifically for children with disabilities
- Partnerships with local foundations and businesses to fund, staff, and run additional learning programs for specific disabilities or gifted children as a part of the district's curriculum
- Subject-specific partnerships to give students, gifted in a specific area, possibilities to continue instruction in a more advanced setting. In addition

to non-core subjects discussed earlier, schools could collaborate with local colleges to secure instruction in some core subjects for students who, regardless of their age, have mastered K–12 curriculum in these subjects.

- Partnerships to afford virtual learning for students who either cannot attend school or require additional challenges

Enrichment-oriented partnerships, focused on providing students with additional opportunities for learning, can include partnerships with individual community organizations, services, libraries, or businesses.

- After-school clubs/activities geared specifically to students with disabilities or the gifted and talented
- On-site tutoring opportunities provided by local tutoring services to students with disabilities
- Camps during school breaks, geared specifically to the needs of gifted children or children with certain disabilities

In addition, care-oriented partnerships that should be considered by special education or gifted and talented committees and local communities are mentoring programs that serve youth with disabilities by matching them with a caring adult mentor; counseling services for gifted and talented youth; community-based care options for disabled students; and anything that could alleviate everyday stress.

There are many young people in America's schools, whose lives are affected by adversity or unrecognized and unmet needs. Some live in poverty; some have little support at home; some have learning or physical disabilities; and some are intellectually gifted but emotionally distraught. On their own, these children are unlikely to reach their full human potential. If society intervenes early and combines various resources to support each child, each child will have a chance for a successful life.

REFLECT ON THIS

For Teachers

1. Do I see families in low-income, rural, or immigrant communities as valuable partners in education of their students?
2. Am I taking extra steps to understand these families and to provide them with help and resources to support their children's learning? Am I stereotyping and assuming what their needs are?

3. Do I visit students' homes when I see a correlation between their achievement and factors related to their family life? What prevents me from going?
4. How often do I ask families for feedback? How can I make it a habit?
5. Do I feel confident in my ability to identify students who might need special education or gifted and talented learning services? How can I improve on this?
6. Do I believe in giftedness and the need for some students to have accelerated learning opportunities early to meet their learning needs? What can I do to help these students and their families?
7. Do I invite parents to observe their special education or gifted student's learning in my classroom? Do I offer these parents resources and information on a regular basis?

For School and District Administrators

1. What ongoing learning opportunities exist in my school or district for low-income and immigrant families?
2. How much time do I dedicate to working with these families? How can I become more intentional?
3. What do I communicate to my staff about working with marginalized families on student learning?
4. Do I require all of the teachers to visit student homes when there is a clear connection between students' performance and factors related to their family life? How can I make this happen?
5. Do I proactively seek various collaborations with community and district organizations to provide solutions and learning opportunities for families in need?
6. Does my school or district have structural barriers that hinder teachers from providing each student with learning according to his or her needs and abilities? How can this be changed?
7. Do my teachers and staff receive regular professional development on identifying learning disabilities and giftedness? What do I need to do to make this a priority?
8. Do I have parent representatives from district Special Education and Gifted and Talented organizations on all of the committees that inform instruction?
9. Do I have district-coordinated social media pages and accounts for families of students with special needs? Whom could I ask to be in charge of them?

Chapter 7 Snapshot: PARTNERS IN SPECIAL NEEDS AND CIRCUMSTANCES

FOCUS AREA	CONCERN	WHAT TO CONSIDER
Poverty and other Adversity Factors	Poor attendance Students may have little support at home. Learning environments may be drastically different from the ones promoting learning. Circumstances may substantially impede performance.	Awareness: State's laws and regulations How attendance affects student learning Resources available to parents to make sure that their child attends school Printed weekly classroom communications and monthly district and school newsletters mailed directly to homes Seeking Engagement: Home visits Comprehensive learning systems— e.g., Parent Academies, Parent Universities, Family Centers Supporting Collaboration: A full-service system of resources and support for students in poverty Student care-oriented partnerships Partnerships to offer students alternative opportunities for learning
Special Needs: Special Education and Gifted and Talented Students	A continuous growth in the number of students with autism, Asperger's syndrome, ADD/ADHD, as well as complex medical needs or physical disabilities Profoundly gifted children are not recognized or supported in mainstream environments. Double special students: identified with special education needs, in addition to being accelerated learners in other areas	Awareness: Diagnosis and diagnosis-specific information and resources Learning strategies and techniques that have proved to improve learning for children with a similar condition Seeking Engagement: Participation and decision-making in Individualized Education Plan (IEP) for both special education and gifted students Opportunities for hands-on learning that would allow parents to support their children learning at home

FOCUS AREA	CONCERN	WHAT TO CONSIDER
		Supporting Collaboration: Official recognition and institutionalization of the fact that there are children who require different learning services Including parent representatives from Special Education and Gifted and Talented organizations in a district's decision making Partnering with parental organizations, in general, and special education (gifted and talented) parent-led councils to provide additional professional learning opportunities to teachers in these areas Connecting parents in similar situations with each other and support and advocacy groups Learning- and enrichment-oriented partnerships to support learning needs of special education and gifted students

Chapter Eight

Stories of Engagement

When working toward a culture of partnerships, it is important to remember that the stages of its formation are just landmarks on the same continuous journey; they are not separate destinations. Educators who nurture a culture of partnerships in their schools, in most cases, simultaneously create awareness, engage families, build supporting structures, and seek opportunities to collaborate.

The five stories of meaningful engagement and collaboration offered in this chapter are good testimony to this. Coming from educators positioned in very different educational settings, the stories of their experiences working with families, nonetheless, show the same dynamics: Engagement doesn't happen without some preliminary awareness nor collaboration happens without engagement, and, consequently, awareness. This holds true regardless of who initiates the process—schools or families.

Principal Adam Scher and his school's Visible Thinking Coordinator, Jenny Rossi, from Way Elementary in Bloomfield Hills, Michigan, arranged a learning opportunity for parents: a grade-level exhibition. Before families were asked to participate in hands-on learning of their own, teachers created preliminary awareness by showing parents a film featuring snapshots of their children's learning.

During Individualized Education Plan meetings, Erika Lusky, a speech-language pathologist from Reuther Middle School in Rochester, Michigan, noticed that many parents expressed a need to better communicate with their non-verbal children. This awareness led to the idea to make parents aware of another way of communication with their children and offered them an opportunity to experience this communication first-hand.

Jennifer Miller, an educator and parent from Columbus, Ohio, began collaboration with her son's teacher by making the teacher aware of the boy's reading struggle and by suggesting more frequent learning feedback. Learning feedback, in turn, kept Miller aware of how her child felt about reading, which allowed her to effectively engage in providing the right help.

Meeting her students' families and becoming aware of their home circumstances made it possible for Bonnie Lathram, an educator and writer at *Getting Smart* in Seattle, Washington, to engage families in students' learning. Partnerships with families, to ensure that children succeed, also developed as results of awareness. In many cases, during teacher home visits, families became aware of their roles in supporting their child's learning in tandem with a teacher, which led to enduring engagement.

Finally, the partnership and collaboration achieved by families and educators of J.O. Wilson Elementary School in Washington, DC, as told by Georgina Ardalan, a preschool teacher, happened as a result of making parents aware of the specific needs of the school and children, removing barriers to their engagement, and sharing power and decision making.

EXHIBITIONS FOR POWERFUL PARENT LEARNING

Adam Scher, Principal, and Jenny Rossi, Visible Thinking Coordinator,

Way Elementary, Bloomfield Hills, Michigan.

The lights are dimmed, and the film runs. The faces of enthusiastic, promising students appear. It's the Third-Grade Visible Thinking Exhibition—one of our grade-level events for parents to see, hear, and experience a story of student learning.

The endeavor of school is learning, and learning is aided through a symbiotic relationship between student, teacher, and parent. The learning for parents begins as early as our kindergarten roundup and continues through the messaging on our website and the distributed articles, all the way to the myriad of individual conversations and learning opportunities like today.

Parents don a different cap today, as the tables are turned and they occupy the role of learners to the teachings of their child. The Throughline "How do we organize our world?" flashes across the screen. A *Throughline* is a grade-specific, recurring motif used in each of our classrooms to help tell a year-long story of learning. This Exhibition's focus is on the process of learning via the immersion of science and language arts to answer two questions:

- How do we organize living things?
- How are expository texts organized?

Underneath the umbrella of the throughline lies the understanding goal: *How do scientists use characteristics for classification?* A hallmark of our work, however, is capturing evidence of understanding not only for our student population but our parent population as well. So there is also another goal here: To give parents an experience that would lead them to understanding our instructional vision and set of beliefs about learning, including

- Focusing students on the learning versus the work
- Teaching for understanding versus mere knowledge
- Encouraging deep versus surface learning strategies
- Promoting independence versus dependence
- Developing a growth versus fixed mindset

The film keeps on rolling. Like the concrete worker who lays the foundation for a house, the teachers first develop in students necessary skills to build upon. Parents see that, as an entry point to the basics of classification, students sort beads. Then, children reason with evidence when examining a Science Court presentation, highlighting the concepts of living, non-living, and dead things. Once they have a secure grasp of this skill, the teachers move the idea of classification to real-world objects. Images of random items, such as a wooden desk, an apple at the store, an egg in a nest, a dog, a flower in a vase, or a stick on the ground, are scattered throughout the classroom; parents watch how students classify these items, build explanations, and justify their sorts.

Now that we have framed a basic understanding, the teachers plumb deeper into the area of living things. The film continues to roll, showing how thinking routines are introduced as tools for going deeper with ideas. The *See, Think, Wonder* thinking routine examining a turtle, a hermit crab, and a snake is employed for three purposes: to slow down the observation process in order to notice and name more detail, to generate questions to be posted for further investigation, and to name and understand how vertebrates and invertebrates fit into the unit of study.

Parents' education continues as they learn how students are organized into five vertebrate groups to begin collective research before narrowing to the individual level. Expository texts are plentiful. There are no textbooks here, as part of the art of teaching is matching the right material with the right reading level. Groups present their findings, and teachers employ the *Connect–Extend–Challenge* thinking routine as a tool for reflection. Listeners capture what was already known, what new learnings have occurred, and what complexities and questions remain.

Now that students are flying solo, the *Question Starts* thinking routine is used to generate wonders regarding Michigan vertebrates. While following their inquiries and reading, students capture the heart of information gleaned into subtopics. At this juncture, teachers model how to write paragraphs from notes. Drafting and editing follow, and text features are included in the final draft of individual books.

The film stops. All of this takes place in the first seven minutes of the Exhibition. Although parents are deeply impressed with the process of learning at play, it's hard for them to assess the value we place on teaching for understanding that goes well beyond memorization and skill building and well beyond learning in isolation.

It's at this point that the teaching to parents transfers from the teacher to the student. Sitting side by side with their parents, students lead them through their own journey, beginning with their initial inquiries, justifying the content choices, showing off their note-taking skills, reflecting on the revisions and edits, and finally celebrating their published piece (a final product). The student-led discussions open a window into further understanding the learning process.

At the Exhibition's end, parents are asked to complete a survey regarding their child's learning. Questions for the survey are based around our set of beliefs and instructional vision, formulated from Ron Ritchhart, an author and the principal investigator of the Visible Thinking framework. Questions on the survey include:

• Did today's Exhibition give you a deeper insight into how students learn at Way Elementary?
• Do you see evidence that supports ownership in your child's learning?
• At home, has your child discussed learning from the Exhibition?
• Was your child capable of explaining his/her learning today?
• Did you witness greater evidence of the learning process or the learning product?

Overwhelmingly, parents provide affirmation of our instructional vision. Exhibitions indicate but one small way to educate our parents of our instructional approach. These types of powerful experiences take place at each grade level, every year. Opening the door to our "home" continues to teach us the power of these relationships.

TEACHING PARENTS TO USE IPADS TO COMMUNICATE WITH NON-VERBAL STUDENTS

Erika Lusky, Speech Pathologist,

Reuther Middle School, Rochester, Michigan

As a speech therapist, my caseload of students can vary. Quite a number of the cognitively impaired children on my caseload have severe communication impairments and are "non-verbal" to some degree. With the assistance of specific programs on an iPad, students are able to express their needs and desires, gain and share information, and build and maintain relationships through the use of "core vocabulary" and additional means of icons, pictures, words, phrases, sentences, and questions.

As I began to attend the Individualized Education Plan (IEP) meetings for the students who utilize iPads, I noticed a trend in parent concerns and hopes for their children: They all expressed a strong desire to better communicate with their children. At the same time, as we shared goals, hopes, and future plans, another trend appeared: None of the parents used their children's iPads at home on a regular or even semi-regular basis for communication. This meant that non-verbal students neither had a substantial input in their learning plan nor communicated their learning to parents. This also meant that parents had a very limited ability to help them learn due to a lack of communication.

There was clearly a disconnect between school and home learning environments. Using iPads could help parents assist their kids with learning and improve students' learning environment at home. Parents had to realize the importance of their child's communication device. To accomplish this, I collaborated with the classroom teacher to have an open classroom event in her classroom to model an hour of the school day for parents and then to provide them with an opportunity to interact with their children using their iPads.

I e-mailed all of the parents whose children were using iPads as their primary means of communication and asked them whether they would be interested in coming to school and exploring in action the learning their children experience in the classroom. All parents responded enthusiastically and showed up; some of them changed their work schedules to attend the event. It was clear that they saw a substantial value in such learning.

We met in the students' classroom: each student's parent(s) by his or her side with the iPad between them. Together, we explored the vocabulary, sequence of pages, and other elements available on their devices. Next, the students engaged in a literature lesson as they normally would. After the lesson, parents and students were invited to interact with one another by using the devices in a less formal manner, just to talk. I walked around, listened, and observed.

Enlightenment filled the room; I could see it on parents' faces. It was evident that parents were not familiar with their children's devices. Although parents did have conversations with their children daily, they honestly admitted that they didn't take the time to do so with their communication device, because it was much quicker and easier to speak verbally and assume (in some cases) what their child needed or wanted. There is definitely a large amount of patience involved in navigating a different language that comes with the specific program. However, they all claimed that they would be much more intentional to include this important piece of technology in their discussions, questions, and decision making in the future.

Since the event, I have noticed an increase in the students' use of their devices while at school as if they attached a special purpose to it. Connecting a purpose between home and school gives learning a perceived worth as it becomes meaningful. I have also noticed an increase in students' ability to comment, answer, share, and engage with peers and adults by using their communication devices. My observations were supported by documented achievement of their IEP goals and objectives as well as documented observations and comments from staff. Some parents have become more familiar with the communication device and the program and are beginning to add or adapt vocabulary to tailor it specifically to their child. Most importantly, the change and growth in students' agency and identity was apparent.

FEEDBACK THAT MATTERS: USING SELF-ASSESSMENTS TO CONNECT PARENTS TO CHILDREN'S LEARNING IN SCHOOL

Jennifer Miller, M.Ed., Social and Emotional Learning Expert,

Columbus, Ohio

"I feel with my whole body that I won't learn to read," muttered my almost first-grade son with a furrowed brow, a look of disappointment, and a hint of expectancy. "Say it isn't so" was included in the subtext of his complex emotions. This was coming from a child who couldn't enter a room in our home (except for the coat closet) without encountering a book shelf filled with stories of dragons, buried treasure, and fantastic adventures.

Perhaps precisely because E., my son, comes from a family of readers, he assigned tremendous weight to the process of learning to read. "If it's an essential part of our lives, what if I just couldn't?" he worried. My first thought was that it was not possible. But then, a second thought crept in, "What if he had a learning challenge like dyslexia? What then?" My third thought wiped worry away: "We'll deal with it. Whatever the challenge, none is so great that it would prevent him from reading eventually."

And so it goes with our children's learning challenges. As parents, we often don't fully understand what they are going through and what supports they are getting at school to help them reach their learning goals. So we do the best we can to reinforce those goals from home. For this particular challenge, I knew I could help, but I didn't know how. We had read together every day since he was born. So what else could I do to encourage his desire to read?

First, his emotions were key to his success. How he felt about his ability to learn, his self-efficacy, was impacting his motivation to put in the practice time: the hard work required to learn anything worthwhile. And the twice-a-year parent–teacher conferences for 10 minutes did not seem adequate feedback for me to understand and support his progress. I couldn't count on his verbal reports, since he offered little to no details. There had to be another way of regularly connecting to his reading progress and supports in school without overburdening the teacher.

During our first parent–teacher conference in October, I communicated these concerns to my son's teacher, who then shared with me a simple self-assessment titled, *How Do You Feel? Self-Evaluation.* On this worksheet, there were outlines of six fish to be colored, labeled "Making Friends," "Math," "Reading," "Listening," "Writing," and "Science." The directions read: "Color green for 'I am good at this,' yellow for 'I am pretty good at this,' and red for 'This is hard for me.'" As I suspected at that time, he had colored his "Reading" fish red.

When I brought the self-evaluation home, sharing it with my son gave me an opening to begin a conversation about his worries. I offered my predictions of what they might be while he let me know whether I was right or wrong. Yes, he was concerned that his friends were reading faster than he was. No, he didn't worry about knowing basic words. He knew them. Yes, he was worried about getting through the text quickly and tended to skip words because of it. No, he didn't need help sounding out most words.

This conversation offered rich insight into how we might practice together at home. I quickly contacted the teacher via e-mail and asked for more frequent access to my son's evaluation of his own progress. It was a simple step for her to give out self-assessments each Friday, have students complete them in a matter of seconds, and send them home in their folders. But for me, it meant regular access to my son's thoughts and feelings about reading. With little effort, it achieved three levels of connection:

- It connected my son to his own feelings and thoughts while reflecting on his learning goals.
- It connected me, the parent, to the classroom curriculum, the teacher, and my child's relationship to both.
- It connected me to my own child's feelings and thoughts about his learning goals.

Teachers have been improving their classroom practices through self-efficacy evaluations based on research for decades. "Personal goal setting is influenced by self-appraisal of capacities. The stronger the perceived self-efficacy, the higher the goal challenges people set for themselves and the firmer the commitment to them" (Bandura, 1993).

For students, research has demonstrated that explicit instruction in meta-cognition—the ability to monitor their own thinking and learning—can lead to learning success across subjects from primary school through college (Wilson & Conyers, 2014). Though students are assessed by schools on learning standards, it is a rare opportunity for them to reflect regularly on their own thoughts and feelings related to their learning goals, even though it can have a positive impact on their motivation and progress.

As for my son and me, the weekly feedback allowed for more detailed conversations about how he was learning. That insight assisted me in becoming more sensitive to problems and avoiding areas that might have made him defensive. Instead, I would focus on the small interventions that supported his goals. For example, I refrained from quickly supplying the word when he was struggling with sounding it out, waiting until he asked for help.

Often, he would struggle through and figure it out himself. If he asked, I would only sound out a syllable to get him started. I found that our time reading together became less of a power struggle and more of an opportunity for a real connection. I watched his red-colored fish ("This is hard for me") turn yellow ("I am pretty good at this") at mid-year. By the third quarter, it was a definitive green: "I am good at this."

REACHING THE FAMILY MEANS
REACHING THE STUDENT

Bonnie Lathram, educator and writer, co-author of *Smart Parents*,

Getting Smart, Seattle, WA

On a cold, rainy day in Seattle, I drove 30 minutes from my house in West Seattle to a McDonald's in Kent, Washington, to meet with a student and his mom. The student was not doing well in school, and our school's principal Loren Demeroutis and I agreed that the best way to find out the cause of it was to get to know the student's family. We made an arrangement to meet the student's mom for breakfast at McDonald's at 6:30 in the morning.

Over Egg McMuffins and coffee, we discussed the student's future aspirations and I played with his younger brother. We heard about family circumstances that were getting in the way of the student's success, taking notes of what could be done by the school to alleviate them. The student's mother said that no other teacher or principal had cared about her son the way that we had.

Although this breakfast took place 10 years ago, I remember clearly that the boy and his mother seemed surprised and amazed that the principal and the teacher would actually make the effort to come to their neighborhood to meet with the family. Loren and I didn't feel like we were doing anything special. We were simply making the time to engage the family and listening—two things at the core of our school's philosophy.

I worked for eight years as an advisor at one of Big Picture Learning schools that was located near Seattle. A public school in the Highline School District, the school emphasized real-world and interest-based learning. At Highline Big Picture School, we honed our approach to parent meetings, using a blend of in-person, in-community, and even the in-home approach, and also regularly invited parents to the school. This approach worked. The graduation rate across the Big Picture Learning network of schools is more than 90%, which is higher than the national average of 82%.

I visited the home of every student in my senior class, all 17 of them. I knew my students' parents by their first name and often had their cell phones saved in my phone. Not only did I have personal connections with the parents but also in many cases I knew members of their extended family and siblings. I am still in regular contact with my students who graduated in 2010. Some of them have college degrees, some are in school now, and some are working. My student Stephanie is pursuing acting; my student Hope is back in school after taking time off to have a child.

There are many stories of successes. The story of the early morning at McDonald's, however, has always stuck with me, because this was a story of failure. This student hasn't graduated. I feel we were too late, and if we had reached that student earlier, perhaps his trajectory would have been different. I was (and am) in this work, because we have to be able to take the long view regarding our work with students and their families. To make sure that every child learns, every child needs to be treated as an individual. In my explorations, as a teacher and now as a parent of two young children, I have learned that parents should play a proactive role in their children's learning, whereas schools have to include them in the planning and assessment of student work and treat them as valued members of the school community.

LETTING PARENTS LEAD: HOW BUILDING A TRIKES' SHED BUILT A PARTNERSHIP AT OUR SCHOOL

Georgina Ardalan, Preschool Teacher,

J.O. Wilson Elementary School, District of Columbia Public Schools, Washington, DC

Trikes are really important to preschool-age children. Not only are they fun to ride, but trikes also increase confidence, provide great exercise, and develop balance. Through the connection of steering and pumping, bilateral coordination is reinforced while pedaling promotes gross motor skills. Sharing a trike builds socio-emotional skills.

The preschool program at J.O. Wilson Elementary School in District of Columbia Public Schools is a Title 1 Head Start program. We discovered that often the trikes at school are the only trikes available to children. There were, however, challenges with accessibility of the trikes. Space is typically an issue in any school, but it is especially the case in urban areas like Capitol Hill in Washington, DC. J.O. Wilson has seven preschool classrooms, with three to four trikes assigned to each classroom. The trikes were disorganized and piled in the cubby area, where they were hard to access and, therefore, rarely used.

In response to the need for improved accessibility, after some research, teachers found that an outdoor shed to store the trikes not only would organize the trikes but also improve accessibility and the likelihood of their use. The teachers' idea became a reality when parents took charge of the project and created a true collaboration between the school, families, businesses, and community organizations.

Four parents–experts—a landscape architect, Matt Arnn, an architect, William Teass, an environmentalist, Jamal Kadri, and an all-around-handy guy, Alex Best—together designed and implemented a concept that went well beyond anything the teachers had imagined: a trike storage with a green roof.

After conceptual sketches were made, the four parents presented them to the principal and to our school's parent–teacher association (PTA), making sure that the entire school community was informed and involved in this project. After the approval, another group of parents took a lead in writing a grant for the materials needed to build a shed and to purchase additional trikes. The Capitol Hill Community Foundation, whose purpose is to help build a stronger and more caring community, stepped in and awarded the school $2,000 for the project.

From there, the torch was picked up by yet another group of enthusiastic parents who began construction work by framing up the shed in a weekend, built strong enough to support 6" of engineered soil saturated with rain. The green roof media required to cover the entire shed was 1.5 cubic yards (2,000 pounds). Stancills, a company that custom mixes engineered soil for green roofs, agreed to donate that amount in a "supersack." Without hesitation, other resourceful parents—Vanessa and Jeff Jordan—rented a U-haul trailer to pick up green roof media from Stancills and delivered it to the school.

Cultivate the City, an organization of volunteer urban farmers working to feed families and communities, worked alongside the intrepid families to shovel the soil from the trailer to the green roof. One of our three-year-old volunteers helped to stomp down the soil. A local bike shop (The Daily Rider) provided the wires to lock the trikes up when not in use. After the construction was finished and the soil was laid, the preschool classrooms took turns planting materials donated by a parent.

The result was much more than a beautiful, eco-friendly, food-producing storage shed for the trikes, serving 125 preschool children. It was also a partnership between families, teachers, and community members who had used their collective resources to give children an experience and learning opportunities that they wouldn't have otherwise had. With commitment, expertise, time, energy, and a belief that it could be done, the school community created an addition to the school that would serve its students well into the future.

> All parents want to help out if they can. Between jobs, kids, life, it's pretty difficult to engage to the extent we'd like. In most cases, parents don't approach teachers with specific ideas about how to improve their classrooms and schools. It's really important that teachers articulate what they need and help navigate the institutional relationships and regs to make it all happen. Whether it's shelves, storage sheds, field trip chaperones, room materials, or other resources, you were incredibly adept at imagining, motivating, and managing these parent partnerships. (Matt Arnn, personal communication)

This is an important insight regarding a teacher's role in forming partnerships between schools and families—something that schools and educators should always remember.

Concluding Thoughts

When considering building powerful learning environments, it is necessary to realize that power comes from the diversity of perspectives, expertise, experiences, and resources. No one person sees all of the needs, knows all of the questions to ask, or has all of the answers. This book was focused on nurturing effective and coherent macro learning environments that typically exist within certain geographical locations and are defined by the proximity to school districts. Comprising many micro learning environments, a macro learning ecosystem provides a holistic foundation for learning and encompasses learning contexts where learners spend most of their time.

Learning, however, doesn't end there. Interconnectedness, which has become one of the predominant features of our times, makes us connected to the world in ways that are hard to fully comprehend. Within local communities, each partnership that schools enter can bring with it more connections and resources than originally anticipated. Every partner is likely to have a network of partners who, in turn, are connected to many other networks and resources. School parent–teacher associations (PTAs), for example, are connected to other school, district, state, and national PTAs; libraries share resources and programs with other libraries and are connected to larger entities; and businesses and foundations are connected to many other businesses and business associations, often globally.

Modern technology takes a learning environment to an entirely new level of networking and collaboration. Global learning experiences are an important part of rigorous education. By utilizing technology and learning platforms, students can experience global learning and enter collaborations with students from all over the world. There are various platforms: for example, Google Hangouts, which allows a one-on-one conversation or group chats for approximately 100 people, or Skype in the Classroom, which connects classrooms from around the globe and brings elements of adventure by taking students on virtual field trips via Skype.

There are many applications (apps), currently used by businesses, students, parents, and educators, that can extend a learning environment well beyond school or home walls:

- Nearpod: a multiplatform that works on every device and allows to create and customize work
- Padlet: a virtual "bulletin" board where participants can collaborate, reflect, and share links and pictures in a secure location
- Kahoot!: a program that promotes social learning by facilitating construction of various learning games played in a group setting, whether in the same classroom or across the ocean
- Google Drive: a place and a tool that can be used for international blogging and collaborative projects
- Periscope: a live video streaming app for iOS and Android that enables users to broadcast live via their mobile devices at any time in any location—streaming video and audio—to any viewers who join the broadcast

Virtual learning that comes from various learning providers can include programs and platforms that are targeted to developing a specific set of skills or reaching specific goals. There are opportunities for business simulation classes that create online scenarios close to real tasks that exist in many industries. Students in competing teams may enact running operations or designing a product that has to meet specific criteria, for example. Even playing video games in a community of players from around the globe provides a context for learning.

This leads to one natural conclusion: When learners simultaneously tap into multiple resources and engage with multiple providers, opportunities and contexts for learning are endless. Building partnerships with families, community organizations and agencies, and learning establishments will enable schools to create synergies, develop new ways to enhance professional and cultural capital of all stakeholders, and nurture a powerful learning ecosystem, thriving on the diversity of perspectives, expertise, experiences, and resources.

References

7 innovative apps for parent-teacher communication [Web log post]. (2015, January 28). Retrieved from http://teach.com/education-technology/parent-teacher-apps

Abbott, J. (2010). *Overschooled but undereducated: How the crisis in education is jeopardizing our adolescents*. London: Continuum International Publishing Group.

Adams, K. S. & Christenson, S. L. (2000). Trust and the family-school relationship: Examination of parent-teacher differences in elementary and secondary grades. *Journal of School Psychology*, 38. 477–497. doi: 10.1016/S0022-4405(00)00048-0

Akyol, Z. & Garrison, D. R. (2013). *Educational Communities of Inquiry: Theoretical framework, research and practice*. Hershey, PA: IGI Global. doi: 10.4018/978-1-4666-2110–17

Arabo, M. (2016, February 5). Separate is not equal [Web log post]. Retrieved from http://www.melodyarabo.com/blog

ASCD. (2007). *The learning compact redefined: A call to action*. Alexandria, VA: Author. Retrieved from http://www.ascd.org/ASCD/pdf/Whole%20Child/WCC%20Learning%20Compact.pdf

Bandura, A. (1993). Perceived self-efficacy in cognitive development and functioning. *Educational Psychologist*. 28(2), 117–148.

Bates, A. W. (2015). *Teaching in a Digital Age*. Canada: BC Open Textbooks. Retrieved from https://opentextbc.ca/teachinginadigitalage/

Bellingham Public Schools. (n.d.). *Parent advisory committee*. Retrieved from https://bellinghamschools.org/projects/parent-advisory-committee/parent-advisory-committee

Blank, M. J. & McGuire, K. (2016). "People support what they create:" Stakeholder engagement is key to ESSA's future. *Education Week*. 35(30), 28; 25.

Boix Mansilla, V. (2013, September 15). Finding our place in the world. *Out of Eden Learn Blog*. Retrieved from https://walktolearn.outofedenwalk.com/2013/12/15/finding-our-place-in-the-world/

Boix Mansilla, V. & Jackson, A. (2011). *Educating for global competence: Preparing our youth to engage the world.* New York, NY: Asia Society. Retrieved from https://asiasociety.org/files/book-globalcompetence.pdf

Bokas, A. A. (Producer). (2014–2016). *The Future of Learning [Television series].* Clarkston, MI: Independence Television. Retrieved from http://www.independencetelevision.com/future-of-learning.html

Bokas, A. A. & Andress, H. (2016, March 24). Coaching parents to communicate lifelong learning. *ASCD Express.* 11(14). Retrieved from http://www.ascd.org/ascd-express/vol11/1114-bokas.aspx

Bokas, A. A. & Rock, R. D. (2015, May 26). Changing the mindset of education: Every learner is unique. *Huffington Post Education.* Retrieved from http://www.huffingtonpost.com/smart-parents/changing-the-mindset-of-e_b_7445856.html

Bradbury, J. & Busch, S. E. (2015). *Empowering families: Practical ways to involve parents in boosting literacy.* New York, NY: Routledge.

Brea Olinda Unified School District. (n.d.). *Mission statement.* Retrieved from http://www.bousd.k12.ca.us/cms/page_view?d=x&piid=&vpid=1264862003362

Bryk, A. S. & Schneider, B. (2003). Trust in schools: A core resource for school reform. *Educational Leadership.* 60(6), 40–45.

Cargile, E. (2016, February 8). Documentary changing way Central Texas schools approach learning. *Kxan.* Retrieved from: http://kxan.com/2016/02/08/dripping-springs-isd-uses-documentary-to-explain-new-vision-for-learning/

Center on the Developing Child. (n.d.). *Early childhood mental life.* Retrieved from http://developingchild.harvard.edu/science/deep-dives/mental-health/

Charlotte-Mecklenburg Schools. (n.d.). *What is Parent University?* Retrieved from http://www.cms.k12.nc.us/parents/ParentUniv/Pages/WhatisParentUniversity.aspx

Chen, J., Ishimaru, A., & Lott, J. (2015, July 28). Designing equitable parent-school collaboration. *Impatient Optimists.* Retrieved from http://www.impatientoptimists.org/Posts/2015/07/Designing-Equitable-ParentSchool-Collaboration#.VzUagGPAdp8

Claxton, G. (2002). *Building learning power: Helping young people become better learners.* Bristol: TLO Limited.

Cohen, S. (2014, March 10). The globalization of education and sustainability management. *Huffington Post.* Retrieved from http://www.huffingtonpost.com/steven-cohen/the-globalization-of-educ_b_4934023.html

Colvin, G. (2014, September 4). Employers are looking for new hires with something extra: Empathy. *Fortune.* Retrieved from http://fortune.com/2014/09/04/employers-new-hires-empathy/

Cutler III, W. (2000). *Parents and schools: The 150-year struggle for control in American education.* Chicago, IL: University of Chicago Press.

Davis, R. (2014, September 24). Embracing student creativity with a wonder shelf. *Edutopia.* Retrieved from http://www.edutopia.org/blog/embracing-student-creativity-wonder-shelf-rafranz-davis

Descartes, R. (1639). *Meditations on First Philosophy.* Retrieved https://www.marxists.org/reference/archive/descartes/1639/meditations.htm

Detroit Public Schools. (2014, February 12). *DPS kicks off registration for new Parent University.* Retrieved from http://detroitk12.org/content/2014/02/12/dps-kicks-off-registration-for-new-parent-university/

Doyle, T. (2011). *Learner-Centered teaching: Putting the research on learning into practice.* Sterling, VA: Stylus Publishing, LLC.

Duckworth, A. L., Peterson, C., Matthews, M. D., & Kelly, D. R. (2007). Grit: Perseverance and passion for long-term goals. *Journal of Personality and Social Psychology.* 92(6), 1087–1101. doi: 10.1080/00223890802634290

Dumont, H., Istance, D., & Benavides, F. (eds.) (2010). *The nature of learning: Using research to inspire practice, educational research and innovation.* Paris, France: OECD Publishing. doi: http://dx.doi.org/10.1787/9789264086487-en

East Syracuse Minoa Schools. (n.d.). *East Syracuse Minoa Central School District Strategic Plan 2013–2018. Priorities 2015–2016.* East Syracuse, NY: Author. Retrieved from http://www.esmschools.org/files/24324/15-16-stretegic-plan-priorities-final.pdf

Educating Our Children Together. (n.d.). Retrieved from http://www.directionservice.org/cadre/pdf/children_strategy_2.pdf

Epstein, J. L. & Salinas, K. C. (2004). Partnering with Families and Communities. *Educational Leaderships.* 61(8), 12–18.

Every Student Succeeds Act of 2015, S.1177, 114th Cong. (2015–2016).

Families in Schools. (2015). *Ready or not: How CA school districts are reimagining parent engagement in the era of Local Control Funding Formula.* Los Angeles, CA: Author. Retrieved from http://www.scusd.edu/sites/main/files/file-attachments/families_in_schools_lcap_report.pdf

Farkas, S. & Duffet, A. (2008). Results from a national teacher survey. In Thomas B. Fordham Institute, *High achievement students in the era of NCLB (p. 78).* Washington, DC: Author. Retrieved from http://www.edexcellence.net/publications/high-achieving-students-in.html

Ferguson, R. (2002). *What doesn't meet the eye: Addressing racial disparities in high-achieving suburban schools.* Oak Brook, IL: North Central Regional Educational Laboratory. Retrieved from http://files.eric.ed.gov/fulltext/ED474390.pdf

Ferlazzio, L. (2016, January 23). Response: "Successful schools solicit" family engagement [Web log post]. *Education Week Classroom Q&A With Larry Ferlazzo Blog.* Retrieved from http://blogs.edweek.org/teachers/classroom_qa_with_larry_ferlazzo/2016/01/response_successful_schools_solicit_family_engagement.html

Findley, M. J. & Cooper, H. M. (1983). Locus of control and academic achievement. *Journal of Personality and Social Psychology.* 44(2), 419–427. doi: 10.1037/0022-3514.44.2.419

Gardner, H. (1995). *Five minds for the future.* Boston, MA: Harvard Business School Press.

Gardner, H. (1999). *Intelligence re-framed: Multiple intelligences for the 21st Century.* New York, NY: Basic Books.

Gardner, H. (2006). *Changing minds: The art and science of changing our own and other people's minds.* Boston, MA: Harvard Business Review Press.

Gardner, H. (2012). *Truth, beauty, and goodness re-framed.* New York, NY: Basic Books.

Gardner, H. & Davis, K. (2013). *The App generation: How today's youth navigate identity, intimacy, and imagination in a Digital World.* New Haven, CT: Yale University Press.

Goals 2000: Educate America Act of 1993. H.R. 1804, 103rd Cong. (1993).

Gordon, D. (2012, June 19). How districts create community connections with social media. *The Journal.* Retrieved from https://thejournal.com/Articles/2012/06/19/how-social-media-creates-connections-for-school-districts.aspx?Page=3

Harnessing the Power of Stories with Jennifer Aaker. (n.d.). *Learn in.* Retrieved from http://cdn-media.leanin.org/wp-content/uploads/2013/03/HarnessingStories3.15.pdf

Harrisburg School District. (n.d.). Retrieved from http://harrisburgdistrict41-2.org/?page_id=2

Henderson, A. T. & Mapp, K. L. (2002). *A new wave of evidence: The impact of school, family, and community connections on student achievement.* Austin, TX: National Center for Family and Community Connections with Schools.

Henderson, A. T., Mapp, K. L., Johnson, V. R., & Davies, D. (2007). *Beyond the bake sale.* New York, NY: The New Press.

Hillmann, P. (2011, April 2). How to support your gifted child's education. *The Washington Family and Community Engagement Trust.* Retrieved from http://www.wafamilyengagement.org/articles/giftedness.html

Horn, M. & Staker, H. (2014). *Blended: Using disruptive innovation to improve schools.* San Francisco, CA: Jossey-Bass.

Horowitz, S. (2015, October 2). This is what the state of freelancing in the U.S. means for the future of work. *Fast Company.* Retrieved from http://www.fastcompany.com/3051686/the-future-of-work/the-state-of-freelancing-in-the-us-in-2015

Hough, L. (2014, September 8). How teachers can make caring more common. *Usable Knowledge.* Retrieved from http://www.gse.harvard.edu/news/uk/14/09/how-teachers-can-make-caring-more-common

How to study and learn, part. 1. (2013). *Foundation for Critical Thinking.* Retrieved form http://www.criticalthinking.org/pages/how-to-study-and-learn-part-one/513

Humboldt Elementary. (2015, April 7). Sharing data to create stronger parent partnerships. *Edutopia.* Retrieved from http://www.edutopia.org/practice/sharing-data-create-stronger-parent-partnerships

Immordino-Yang, M. H. (2008). The smoke around mirror neurons: Goals as sociocultural and emotional organizers of perception and action in learning. *Mind, Brain, and Education.* 2(2), 67–73. doi: 10.1111/j.1751-228X.2008.00034.x

Immordino-Yang, M. H. (2011). Implications of affective and social neuroscience for educational theory. *Educational Philosophy and Theory.* 43(1), 98–103. doi: 10.1111/j.1469-5812.2010.00713.xl

Immordino-Yang, M. H. & Fisher K. W. (2010). Neuroscience bases of learning. In V. G. Aukrust (Ed.), *International Encyclopedia of Education, 3rd Edition.* (pp. 310–316) Oxford: Elsevier.

James, C. (2014). *Disconnected: Youth, new media, and the ethics gap.* Cambridge, MA: MIT.

James, W. (1884). What is an emotion? *Mind.* 9(34), 188–205. Retrieved from http://www.communicationcache.com/uploads/1/0/8/8/10887248/what_is_an_emotion_-_william_james.pdf

Jatkevicius, J. (2010). Libraries and the lessons of abilene. *Library Leadership & Management.* 24(3), 77–81. Retrieved from: https://journals.tdl.org/llm/index.php/llm/article/viewFile/1845/1118

Jensen, E. (2008). *Brain-based learning: The new paradigm of teaching.* Thousand Oaks, CA: Corwin Press.

Katy Independent School District. (n.d.). *About Katy ISD.* Retrieved from http://www.katyisd.org/Pages/About-KatyISD.aspx

Keeley, B. (2007). *Human capital: How what you know shapes your life.* Paris, France: OECD. doi: 10.1787/9789264029095-en

Kegan, R. & Lahey, L. L. (2009). *Immunity to change: How to overcome it and unlock the potential in yourself and your organization.* Boston, MA: Harvard Business School Publishing.

Khadaroo, T. (2014, November 17). Child homelessness surges to nearly 25 million. *Readers Supported News.* Retrieved from: http://readersupportednews.org/news-section2/318-66/27015-child-homelessness-surges-to-nearly-25-million

Kierkegaard, S. (2009). *Concluding unscientific postscript to the philosophical crumbs.* Cambridge, CA: Cambridge University Press. Retrieved from http://users.clas.ufl.edu/burt/KierkegaardConcludingUnscientificPostscript.pdf

Kochhar-Bryant, C. (1997). Effective collaboration for educating the whole child. *Sage Publications.* Retrieved from http://www.sagepub.com/upm-data/34869_Kochhar_Bryant__Effective_Collaboration_for_Educating_the_Whole_Child_Ch1.pdf

Konrath, S. H., O'Brien, E. H., & Hsing, C. (2011). Changes in dispositional empathy in American college students over time: A meta-analysis. *Personality and Social Psychology Review.* 15(2), 180–198. doi: 10.1177/1088868310377395

Kozol, J. (2005). *The shame of the nation: The restoration of apartheid schooling in America.* New York, NY: Three Rivers Press.

Lakeview Elementary School. (n.d.). *Parent lending library.* Retrieved from http://lakeview.sd54.org/parent-lending-library/

Lamont, M., Boix Mansilla, V., & Sato, K. (2016, May 3). "Optimally ambiguous exchanges" and other Conditions for productive interdisciplinary collaboration. *Social Science Research Council. Items.* Retrieved from http://items.ssrc.org/optimally-ambiguous-exchanges-and-other-conditions-for-productive-interdisciplinary-collaboration/

Lang, A. (2012). *The power of why: Simple questions that lead to success.* New York, NY: Harper Collins Publishers Ltd.

Learning Disabilities Association of America. (n.d.). *Types of Learning Disabilities.* Retrieved from http://ldaamerica.org/types-of-learning-disabilities/

Linkner, J. (2014). *The Road to Reinvention: How to Drive Disruption and Accelerate Transformation.* San Francisco, CA: Jossey-Bass.

Locke, J. (1839). *An essay concerning human understanding.* London: T. Tegg and Son. Retrieved from https://books.google.com

Locus of Control. (n.d.). Retrieved from http://www.oakland.edu/upload/docs/Instructor%20Handbook/Locus%20of%20Control.pdf

Madrazo, C. & Senge, P. (2011). *Being the change: Building communities of collaboration and co-inspiration for systemic change.* Retrieved from http://www.solonline.org/?Readings

Mapp, K. L. (2015). Foreword. In Families in Schools. *Ready or not: How CA school districts are reimagining parent engagement in the era of Local Control Funding Formula (p.3).* Los Angeles, CA: Author. Retrieved from http://www.scusd.edu/sites/main/files/file-attachments/families_in_schools_lcap_report.pdf

Marcus, J. (2012). The poverty gap. *Harvard Education Letter.* 28(4). Retrieved from http://hepg.org/hel-home/issues/28_4/helarticle/the-poverty-gap_539#home

Martinez, S. L. & Stager, G. S. (2013). *Invent to learn: Making, tinkering, and engineering the classroom.* Torrance, CA: Constructing Modern Knowledge Press.

Morris, A., Ross, W., Hosseini, H, & Ulieru, M. (n.d.). Modeling culture with complex, multi-dimensional, multi-agent systems. *The Impact Institute.* Retrieved from http://theimpactinstitute.org/Publications/armlab_culture_chapter_311210.pdf

National Center for Education Statistics. (2015). *Fast facts. Students with disabilities.* Retrieved from https://nces.ed.gov/fastfacts/display.asp?id=64

National School Public Relations Association. (2011, August 26). *National survey pinpoints communication preferences in school communication.* Rockville, MD: Author. Retrieved from https://www.nspra.org/files/docs/Release%20on%20CAP%20Survey.pdf

Neighmond, P. (2013, December 2). School stress takes a toll on health, teens and parents say. *NPR.* Retrieved from http://www.npr.org/blogs/health/2013/12/02/246599742/school-stress-takes-a-toll-on-health-teens-and-parents-say

No Child Left Behind (NCLB) Act of 2001, Pub. L. No. 107–110, § 115, Stat. 1425 (2002).

Noel, A., Stark, P., & Redford, J. (2015). *Parent and family involvement in education, from the National Household Education Surveys Program of 2012 (NCES 2013-028.REV).* Washington, DC: U.S. Department of Education. Retrieved from http://nces.ed.gov/pubs2013/2013028rev.pdf

Novi Community Schools. (n.d.). Retrieved from http://www.novi.k12.mi.us

NPR, Robert Wood Johnson Foundation, & Harvard School of Public Health. (2013, September). *Education and health in schools: A survey of parents summary.* Retrieved from http://media.npr.org/documents/2013/dec/rwjf_npr_harvard_edpoll.pdf

OECD. (2015). *Schooling re-designed: Towards innovative learning systems. Educational Research and Innovation.* Paris, France: OECD Publishing. doi: 10.1787/9789264245914-en

OECD. (2016). *Low-performing students: Why they fall behind and how to help them succeed.* PISA. Paris, France: OECD Publishing. doi: 10.1787/9789264250246-en

Parent University. (n.d.). *Grand Rapids Public Schools and Believe 2 Become.* Retrieved from https://parents.grps.org

Partnership for 21st Century Skills. (n.d.). *21st Century learning environments.* Retrieved from: http://www.p21.org/storage/documents/le_white_paper-1.pdf

Perkins, D. N. (2014). *Future wise: Educating our children for a changing world.* San Francisco, CA: Jossey-Bass.

Perkins, D. N. & Reese, J. D. (2014). When change has legs. *Educational Leadership.* 71(8), 42–47.

Pierce, D. (2016, January 24). 5 Keys to forging strong parental engagement. *Getting Smart.* Retrieved from http://gettingsmart.com/2016/01/five-keys-to-forging-strong-parent-engagement/

Post, G. (2015, August 1). Tips for parents of gifted children: What most parents wish they had known. *Gifted Challenges.* Retrieved from http://giftedchallenges.blogspot.com/2015/08/tips-for-parents-of-gifted-children.html?m=1

Quintero, E. (2014, April 30). We can't just raise expectations. *Albert Shanker Institute.* Retrieved from http://www.shankerinstitute.org/blog/we-cant-just-raise-expectations

Race to the Top Act of 2011. H.R. 1532, 112th Cong. (2012).

Rain Chandler, A. (2015, June 29). Teachers really need to work with families. *Middle Web.* Retrieved from http://www.middleweb.com/23377/teachers-really-need-to-work-with-families/

Ravitch, D. (2013). *Reign of error: The hoax of the privatization movement and the danger to America's public schools.* New York, NY: Knopf.

Ravitch, D. (2014, November 8). Alan Singer: A brief history of the school-to-prison pipeline [Web log post]. Retrieved from http://dianeravitch.net/2014/11/08/alan-singer-a-brief-history-of-the-school-to-prison-pipeline/

Ravitch, D. (2014, November 20). The myth of Chinese super schools. *New York Books.* Retrieved from http://www.nybooks.com/articles/archives/2014/nov/20/myth-chinese-super-schools/

Rebell, M. A. (2012). The right to Comprehensive Educational Opportunity. *Harvard Civil Rights—Civil Liberties Law Review, Harvard Law School.* 47(1), 49–115. Retrieved from http://harvardcrcl.org/wp-content/uploads/2012/03/Rebell.pdf

Reimers, F. (2009). International perspectives on the goals of universal basic and secondary education. In Joel E. Cohen and Martin B. Malin (Eds.), *International perspectives on the goals of universal basic and secondary education* (pp. 183–202). New York, NY: Routledge.

Ripley, A. (2013). *The smartest kids in the world and how they got there.* New York, NY: Simon and Schuster Paperbacks.

Ritchhart, R. (2002). *Intellectual character: What it is, why it matters, and how to get it.* San Francisco, CA: Jossey-Bass.

Ritchhart, R. (2015). *Creating cultures of thinking: The 8 forces we must master to truly transform our schools.* San Francisco, CA: Jossey-Bass.

Ritchhart, R., Church, M., & Morrison, K. (2011). *Making thinking visible: How to promote engagement, understanding, and independence for all learners.* San Francisco, CA: Jossey-Bass.

Robinson, K. & Aronica, L. (2014). *Finding your element: How to discover your talents and passions and transform your life.* New York, NY: Penguin Books.

Robinson, K. & Aronica, L. (2015). *Creative schools: The Grassroots Revolution that's transforming education.* New York, NY: Penguin Books.

Rock, R. & Bokas, A. (2015, March 7). Disrupting education: Capturing the essence. *Brilliant or Insane*. Retrieved from http://www.brilliant-insane.com/2015/03/disrupting-education-capturing-the-essence.html

Rockström, J., Steffen, W., Noone, K., Persson, Å., Chapin III, F. S., Lambin, E. F., Lenton, T. M., Scheffer, M., Folke, C., Schellnhuber, H. J., Nykvist, B., de Wit, C. A., Hughes, T., van der Leeuw, S., Rodhe, H., Sörlin, S., Snyder, P. K., Costanza, R., Svedin, U., Falkenmark, M., Karlberg, L., Corell, R. W., Fabry, V. J., Hansen, J., Walker, B., Liverman, D., Richardson, K., Crutzen, P., & Foley, J. A. (2009). A safe operating space for humanity. *Nature. 461*, 472–475. doi: 10.1038/461472a

Rotherham, A. J. (2011, March 10). Getting the best info on a potential new school. *Times Magazine*. Retrieved from http://content.time.com/time/nation/article/0,8599,2058069,00.html

Rousseau, J. (1979). *Emile, or On education*. (A. Bloom, Trans.). New York, NY: Basic Books, 37.

Samuels, C. (2016). Number of U.S. students in special education ticks upward. *Education Week*. 35(28), 1; 12.

Schleicher, A. (2016). Foreword. In OECD. *Low-performing students: Why they fall behind and how to help them succeed* (pp. 3–4). PISA. Paris, France: OECD Publishing. doi: 10.1787/9789264250246-en

Seligman, M. (1992). *Helplessness: On depression, development, and death*. New York, NY: W. H. Freeman & Company.

Senge, P. M. (2006). *The fifth discipline. The art and practice of a learning organization*. New York, NY: Doubleday.

Senge, P. M., Cambron-McCabe, N., Lucas, T., Smith, B., & Dutton., J. (2012). *Schools that learn: A fifth discipline fieldbook for educators, parents, and everyone who cares about education (Updated and Revised)*. New York, NY: Crown Publishing Group.

Shermer, M. (2012). *The believing brain: From ghosts and gods to politics and conspiracies—how we construct beliefs and reinforce them as truths*. New York, NY: Henry Holt and Company, LLC.

Shwab, K. (2016, January 14). The Fourth Industrial Revolution: What it means, how to respond. *World Economic Forum*. Retrieved from http://www.weforum.org/agenda/2016/01/the-fourth-industrial-revolution-what-it-means-and-how-to-respond

Stets, J. E. & Burke, P. J. (2000). *A Sociological approach to self and identity*. Retrieved from http://wat2146.ucr.edu/papers/02a.pdf.

Stewart, V. (2012). *A world-class education: Learning from international models of excellence and innovation*. Alexandria, VA: ASCD.

Taylor, J. (2011, July 27). Is technology stealing our (self) identities? *Huffington Post*. Retrieved from http://www.huffingtonpost.com/dr-jim-taylor/is-technology-stealing-ou_b_910544.html

Taylor, K. (2015, September 8). A door-to-door push to get parents involved at struggling schools. *The New York Times*. Retrieved from http://www.nytimes.com/2015/09/09/nyregion/a-door-to-door-push-to-get-parents-involved-at-struggling-schools.html

Teaching for Change. (n.d.). *Parent engagement. Tellin' our story: How Tellin' Stories works in school.* Retrieved from http://www.teachingforchange.org/parent-organizing/parent-engagement

The Research & Policy Committee of the Committee for Economic Development. (2006). *Education for global leadership.* Washington, DC: Committee for Economic Development. Retrieved from https://www.ced.org/pdf/Education-for-Global-Leadership.pdf

Tishman, S. & Palmer, P. (2007). Works of art are good things to think about. In Centre Pompidou, *Evaluating the impact of arts and cultural education* (pp. 89–101). Paris, France: Author. Retrieved from http://www.visiblethinkingpz.org/VisibleThinking_html_files/07_Whats_New/WorksOfArt.pdf

Tschannen-Moran, M. (2014). *Trust matters: Leadership for successful schools.* San Francisco, CA: Jossey-Bass.

UNESCO. (2002, June 6). The City Montessori School (India) awarded the 2002 UNESCO prize for Peace Education. [Press Release No.2002-37]. Retrieved from http://linkis.com/www.unesco.org/bpi/e/zI132

United States. (1983). *A nation at risk: The imperative for educational reform: a report to the Nation and the Secretary of Education, United States Department of Education.* Washington, DC: The Commission. Retrieved from https://www2.ed.gov/pubs/NatAtRisk/risk.html

The U.S. Bureau of Labor Statistics. (2014, August 26). *Displaced Workers summary.* Retrieved from http://www.bls.gov/news.release/disp.nr0.htm

U.S. Department of Education. (n.d.). *Programs. Improving basic programs operated by local educational agencies (Title I, Part A).* Retrieved from http://www2.ed.gov/programs/titleiparta/index.html

Vander Ark, T. (2016, February 17). What learning will look like in 2035. *Getting Smart.* Retrieved from http://gettingsmart.com/2016/02/64273/

Variety Child Learning Center. (n.d.). *Open-School policy.* Retrieved from http://www.vclc.org/about/open-door-policy.html

Virginia Beach City Public Schools. (n.d.). Retrieved from http://www.vbschools.com

Vygotsky, L. S. (1978). *Mind in society.* Cambridge, MA: Harvard.

Wagner, T. & Dintersmith, T. (2015). *Most likely to succeed: Preparing our kids for new innovation era.* New York, NY: Scribner.

Warger, T. & Dobbin, G. (2009). *Learning environments: Where space, technology, and culture converge. EDUCAUSE Learning Initiative.* Retrieved from https://net.educause.edu/ir/library/pdf/ELI3021.pdf

Warshaw, D. A. (2011, July 4). Pulling off the ultimate career makeover. *Fortune,* 70–82.

Warshaw, D. A. (2011, July 12). The age of disruption. *The Alden Curve.* Retrieved from http://thewarshawcurve.com/the-age-of-disruption/

Washor, E. (2014, November 17). Washor: Transforming schools in the 21st Century—what makes the difference? *Partnership for 21st Century Skills.* Retrieved from http://www.p21.org/news-events/p21blog/1539-washor-transforming-schools-in-the-21st-century-what-makes-the-difference

Wegerif, R. (2010). *Mind expanding: Teaching for thinking and creativity in primary education*. Berkshire, England: Open University Press.

Weiss, A. R. & Westmoreland, H. (2006). Family and community engagement in Boston Public Schools: 1995–2006. In S. P. Reville & C. Coggins (Eds.), *A decade of urban school reform: Persistence and progress in the Boston Public Schools* (pp. 219–242). Cambridge, MA: Harvard Education Press.

Wheatley, M. (2000). Disturb me, please! [Web log post]. Retrieved from http://www.margaretwheatley.com/articles/pleasedisturb.html

Whitebread, D. (2014, September 24). School starting age: Evidence. *Cambridge University*. Retrieved from http://www.cam.ac.uk/research/discussion/school-starting-age-the-evidence

WIJABA. (n.d.). *Parent libraries*. Retrieved from http://wijaba.org/parent-libraries/

Williamson, B. (2014, December 8). Computing brains: Neuroscience, machine intelligence and big data in the cognitive classroom. *Digital Media + Learning*. Retrieved from http://dmlcentral.net/computing-brains-neuroscience-machine-intelligence-and-big-data-in-the-cognitive-classroom/

Wilson, D. & Conyers, M. (2014). The boss of my brain. *Educational Leadership*. 72(2). http://www.ascd.org/publications/educational-leadership/oct14/vol72/num02/£The-Boss-of-My-Brain£.aspx

Wisconsin Rapids Public School District. (2013, April 15). *Gifted and Talented Educational Services Plan*. Retrieved from http://media.wrps.org/pdf/Gifted_Talented_Educational_Plan.pdf

Zhao, Y. (2009). *Who's afraid of the big bad dragon? Why China has the best (and worst) education system in the World*. San Francisco, CA: Jossey-Bass.

Zhao, Y. (2012). *World class learners: Educating creative and entrepreneurial students*. Thousand Oaks, CA: Corwin Press.

Index

About the Author

Arina Bokas, PhD, is an educator, a parent, a leader, and a thinker. She is the editor and the vice president of *Kids' Standard* Magazine and the producer of *The Future of Learning* public television series with Independence Television in Clarkston, Michigan. She is a faculty member in the department of English at Mott Community College and a member of the Michigan parent–teacher association's (PTA's) Nominating and Leadership Development Committee.

In the past, she served as the president and vice president of Clarkston Community Schools' PTA Council and Bailey Lake Elementary PTA. She presented on school–parent–community partnerships at Harvard's *Project Zero* conferences nationally and internationally and moderated #MichEd and #Hack Learning Twitter chats on partnerships with families. Arina Bokas can be followed on *Twitter* at @arinabokas or on her website at http://culturesofpartnerships.com.

41149455R00111

Made in the USA
Middletown, DE
04 April 2019